What People Are Saying About
The Problem With Christianity

"If you are a thinking person, there are probably some things about Christianity that bother you, maybe even trouble you; and that's true whether you are part of the Christian community or outside it. This book directly confronts a number of these issues in a clear and accessible way. People who read this will grow both in their understanding of Christianity and their knowledge of these hot button issues, and they will see the two being brought together in an engaging and compassionate way. I highly recommend this book."

- Dr. Paul Chamberlain
Director of Trinity Western University's Institute of Christian Apologetics
Author of *Why People Don't Believe: Confronting Seven Challenges to Christian Faith*

"Here is an accessible, pastorally sensitive, and theologically robust guide to answering some of the most common objections to Christianity in our secular age. Barton Priebe's winsome presentation of biblical truth serves as a model of cultural engagement."

- Trevin Wax
Managing Editor of The Gospel Project
Author of *Gospel-Centered Teaching, Clear Winter Nights,*
and *Counterfeit Gospels*; blogger at Kingdom People

"My appreciation and respect for Barton Priebe are encapsulated in this book, one written not by someone sitting in an ivory tower of academia but by a practitioner and Pastor. As a fellow Pastor serving on the west coast of Canada, I cannot tell you how much I appreciate the combination of courage, thoughtfulness and theological astuteness in addressing the topics he does, evidencing all along a great love for people. If your desire is to be equipped, practically and effectively, to respond to those who resist the message of Jesus then I heartily recommend this book to you."

- Norm Funk
Lead Pastor, Westside Church, Vancouver
Author of *Questions Jesus Asked*

"I warmly commend this book by Barton Priebe. His topic is both timely and critical. The tough questions being posed in the culture today urgently need answers like those offered here - respectful, informed and persuasive. These chapters should be required reading for Christians, as well as being passed, as appropriate, into the hands of friends, colleagues, and neighbours."

- Dr. Bruce Milne
Author of *Know The Truth: A Handbook of Christian Belief*

"Christianity has always been subject to scrutiny, but perhaps now more than ever. Barton Priebe, as a working inner city pastor, faces this scrutiny every day. Rather than avoiding the "problems" people have with Christianity, he has chosen to address them directly. *The Problem with Christianity* is not the last word on these challenges, but it is a good word. Priebe speaks to the questions truthfully, but also graciously, as one should expect from a follower of Jesus. Even if you struggle to agree with his conclusions, you will be glad you were helped to understand them. You might even find they are compelling."

- Dr. Kenton C. Anderson
President, Northwest Baptist Seminary; Professor of Homiletics,
ACTS Seminaries of Trinity Western University
Author of *Choosing to Preach*

"In this secular age, we no longer turn to God for meaning and significance. Our modern society has created webs of meaning, but they never adequately provide all the significance we need. *The Problem with Christianity* interacts with the questions posed by a modern society against the Christian Faith. Barton's responses are thoughtful, devoid of cliché, and get to the heart of what the Bible teaches. Read this book, consider these alternative answers, and ask yourself, "Does the world truly answer my deepest questions and longings?"

- Francois Turcotte
Executive Director, SEMBEQ (Séminaire Baptiste Évangélique du Québec)

"I loved this book. It excites me to see Barton defending orthodox Christianity in a way that is engaging with pop culture, respectful of differing worldviews and clearly articulating the truths we evangelicals stand on. With the heart of a pastor and the mind of a scholar, Barton Priebe has given a fantastic defense to some very challenging topics. As a pastor and Christian apologist, I will devour this resource and reference it often. As a Canadian, I am proud to endorse *The Problem With Christianity*."

- Jon Morrison
Lead Pastor, Maple Ridge Baptist Church
Author of *Clear Minds & Dirty Feet: A Reason to Hope, A Message to Share*

THE PROBLEM WITH CHRISTIANITY

SIX UNSETTLING QUESTIONS YOU HAVE ASKED

BARTON PRIEBE

To Heather (Prov 31:29),
Emily, Tyler, Jessica, and Joshua (Ps 127:3)

The Problem with Christianity: Six Unsettling Questions You Have Asked

Published by:
Apologetics Canada Publishing
Abbotsford, BC, Canada.
www.apologeticscanada.com

Cover photo and design by Courteney Chu

Author photo by Beth Gonzalez (Life's Journey Photography)

ISBN-13: 978-1511756280

ISBN-10: 1511756284

CONTENTS

ACKNOWLEDGEMENTS

I want to thank my parents, Glen and Carol Priebe, who were the first ones to encourage me to write. I am very grateful for the people of Dunbar Heights Baptist Church whose questions, discussions, and encouragement over thirteen years have shaped and sharpened me. Many thanks to Dr. Craig Mitton, Dr. Bruce Milne, Dr. Paul Chamberlain, William Badke, Trevin Wax, and Mark McEwan for their constructive criticism on the manuscript and to Joan Newton for her expertise in editing (as authors often point out, any remaining faults are my own). I'm grateful to Jon Morrison for his practical advice on publishing. Thanks to Courteney Chu for her continual support of my ministry, particularly in her artistic design skills. I am very thankful to my wife Heather and my children for their love and support and for allowing me the necessary evenings and weekends to write this book.

PREFACE

When the topic of Christianity comes up in conversation, it is common for someone to say, "The problem with Christianity is..." and then complete the sentence with what he or she believes is the greatest problem with the Christian faith. This is typically expressed with some degree of feeling because "the problem" is something that unsettles the person and thus stands as an obstacle to faith.

One individual may say, "The problem with Christianity is that it is unscientific. How can anyone believe in miracles in an age of science? Another person may have no difficulties with miracles but says, "The problem with Christianity is its teaching on homosexuality. How can anyone believe in a God who is against gay people?" Still another may say, "The problem with Christianity is God himself. Why would I ever want to follow a God who commanded genocide in the Old Testament?" Yet another person will say, "The problem with Christianity is its exclusivity. In a world with such diverse beliefs, how can there possibly be only one way to God?"

It is not just unbelievers who find these questions unsettling. Many believers also struggle to answer such questions and often feel ill equipped to discuss them, especially with those who are not Christians.

Over the past seventeen years I have had the privilege of interacting with many believers and unbelievers who have not been shy in sharing their difficulties with the Christian faith. I spent four years working with students at Trinity Western University and thirteen years pastoring a multicultural urban church located right next to the University of British Columbia on the west side of Vancouver. I presently serve as the lead pastor of Central Baptist Church in Victoria, British Columbia. After many years of campus dialogues, coffee shop conversations, post-service Q/A interactions, and informal discussions, I have found that certain "problems" are raised more often than others. The purpose of this book is to engage six of the most common problems people have with Christianity. I have tried to write each one as a popular level introduction to the subject. It is my hope that these short chapters will inspire readers to move on to book length treatments of those topics of particular interest.

Whether you have been a Christian for many years, are skeptical of Christianity, or would like to interact further on these big questions, it is my hope that *The Problem With Christianity* will prove to be a valuable resource in your thinking and conversations with others.

PROBLEM #1:
HOMOSEXUALITY & GOD

WHY DOES GOD SEEM TO BE AGAINST GAY PEOPLE?

INTRODUCTION

The relationship of Christianity to homosexuality is a big topic in culture today. It is almost impossible to have a discussion about the Christian faith without someone raising questions about it. This makes sense because this is not simply a political or religious topic that we can speak of with a sense of detachment; this is a deeply personal topic. We are talking about real people who often face rejection, bullying, and inner turmoil for identifying as gay.

I begin *The Problem With Christianity* with this subject, not because it is my hobbyhorse, but simply because it is arguably the biggest problem many people have with Christianity. When someone finds out that I am a Christian, one of the first questions they will ask is, "What do you think about homosexuality?" I know that my response will, to a large degree, shape the person's view not only of me but also of the Christian faith I represent. A perceived anti-gay bias keeps them from giving it any further consideration.

The next four chapters will deal with the perception that God seems to be against gay people. I will seek to answer the question, "Is God anti-gay?" These chapters are not meant to be a comprehensive treatment of Christianity and homosexuality; there are many more things that could be said. I aim to stick close to the question at hand and avoid taking too many detours into the many other questions that arise around this topic. Specifically, I want to develop the Bible's answer to whether God is anti-gay in four chapters. In chapter 1 we will talk about the God who is radically inclusive. Next we will discuss the God who revolutionizes identity. In chapter 3 we will explore the God who gives liberating boundaries. Finally, in chapter 4, we will dive into the topic of the God who loves sacrificially.

Chapter 1
The God Who Is Radically Inclusive

There is no question the gay community has felt that God is anti-gay because religious people often act in ways that are anti-gay. Religious people can be very self-righteous and cruel. We have seen the supposed "Christians" who picket with signs that say God hates gay people. We have also heard stories of Christian parents rejecting their children when they find out they are gay.

In their book *unChristian: What a New Generation Really Thinks About Christianity...And Why It Matters*, Barna Group researchers David Kinnaman and Gabe Lyons describe how young people today view the church.

> In our research, the perception that Christians are "against" gays and lesbians...has reached critical mass. The gay issue has become the "big one," the negative image most likely to be intertwined with Christianity's reputation. It is also the dimension that most clearly demonstrates the unChristian faith to young people today, surfacing a spate of negative perceptions: judgmental, bigoted, sheltered, right-wingers, hypocritical,

insincere, and uncaring. Outsiders say our hostility toward gays –
not just opposition to homosexual politics and behaviors but
disdain for gay individuals – has become virtually synonymous
with the Christian faith.[1]

In order to properly answer the question, "Is God anti-gay?"
we must look at two aspects of the larger story of the Bible that
reveal the radical inclusivity of God toward the gay community.

MADE IN THE IMAGE OF GOD

First, the Bible's teaching about God's creation of human
beings reveals the radical inclusivity of God. Genesis 1 says that
when God created human beings he created us to be different
from everything else. Genesis 1:27 says, "So God created man
in his own image, in the image of God he created him; male
and female he created them."

Since man and woman were created in the image of God,
human beings reflect God himself. No animals, fish, or stars
are described as being created in the image of God. Later, in
Genesis 9, God forbids murder on the grounds that people are
made in his image. So to bully, humiliate, or use violence
against a person because they are gay is rightfully understood as
an attack on God himself, because that person is made in
God's image. Whether you are a Christian or not, this should
be welcome news, for the Bible teaches that since all people are
created in the image of God, all people (regardless of sexual
orientation) must be treated with dignity, value, and respect.

---

[1] David Kinnaman and Gabe Lyons, *unChristian: What a New Generation Really Thinks About Christianity…And Why It Matters* (Grand Rapids: Baker Books, 2007), 92.

EQUAL AT THE FOOT OF THE CROSS

Second, the Bible's teaching about Jesus' death on the cross also reveals the radical inclusivity of God. In fact, nowhere is this radical inclusivity of God more on display than at the cross of Jesus. The reason for this is that Jesus receives everyone equally – the ground *is* level at the foot of the cross. The cross declares on the one hand that "there is no one righteous, no not one...for all have sinned."[2] But the cross also declares that Jesus came to die for the sins of all types of people.[3] He came to pay the penalty that we deserve to pay for our sins so that, as John 3:16 asserts, "whoever believes in him will not perish but have eternal life." There is no more inclusive word than "whoever." The word "whoever" necessarily includes everyone – whether lesbian, gay, bisexual, transsexual, queer, white, black, Chinese, Japanese, old, young, rich, or poor. Therefore, since all people are sinners and God gave His Son to rescue sinners, all people are welcome at the foot of the cross.

IMPLICATIONS FOR CHRISTIANS

Thus, it is clear that Christians have much to repent of in regard to our attitudes and behaviours toward the gay community. Jesus saved his harshest words for the self-righteous religious people of his day.

It is my hope, right from the start, that those who are not Christians can see that the Bible purports an inclusivity that is sadly missed when we look at the self-righteous actions of far too many people today. Clearly, this radical inclusivity of God has massive implications, particularly for Christians. For example:

---

[2] Romans 3:18, 23.
[3] Sin is our failure to measure up to God's design for us.

- How can we say we are saved by the sheer grace of God and then act as if we are morally superior to those in the gay community?

- How can we worship our Saviour who treated all people with dignity and yet make jokes that demean gay people?

- Does not Jesus' parable of the Good Samaritan show us that all Christians are duty bound to love and serve their neighbour, regardless of whether that neighbour shares our Christian beliefs or not?[4]

- The Christian view on gender and sexuality is generally well known, but can the same be said for our acts of kindness and compassion toward those within the gay community?

Is God anti-gay? Does God hate gay people? Let me say it plainly – no. God is not anti-gay. God does not hate gay people. All people are made in his image and all people are welcome at the foot of the cross. This is the God who is radically inclusive.

---

[4] See Luke 10:25-37. Jesus tells this parable to a Jewish teacher of the law who seeks to justify himself as one who loves his neighbour. In this parable Jesus tells of a Samaritan man who, at cost to himself, assists a Jewish man who has been robbed, beaten, and left for dead. Jews despised Samaritans in part for their differing religious beliefs. Jesus is therefore challenging his listeners with the idea that loving their neighbours means loving those outside their own belief system.

Chapter 2
The God Who Revolutionizes Identity

"OK," someone says, "we acknowledge that the Bible criticizes self-righteous religious people. We also see that God is not anti-gay in that he says gay people should be treated with respect. We like that. But if you are now going to say that God opposes homosexual behaviour then God *is* anti-gay, for wouldn't he then be telling gay persons to go against the very core of who they are? Telling someone to deny their true identity would most certainly be anti-gay."

In this second chapter I want to show that God cares more about the *core identity* of people, gay or straight, than we can possibly imagine.

THE HUMAN DESIRE FOR FULLNESS OF LIFE

There is no question that most gay people do not choose to experience same sex attraction in the same manner that a person chooses to take up some hobby. This is obviously also true for a straight person in their attraction for the opposite sex. Most gay people state that they have always felt attraction to the same sex. Based on this fact our culture says, "Your same sex attraction tells you who you really are as a person. Your identity is that of a homosexual person. Further, to deny, or go against, the core of your identity will ultimately dehumanize you. Therefore, if you want to be fully human, you need to act on your desires by pursuing same sex relationships."

For example, Lady Gaga's song *Born This Way* says, "No matter gay, straight, or bi, Lesbian, transgendered life...I'm on the right track baby, I was born this way." And Macklemore and Lewis' Grammy nominated song *Same Love* has a woman sing of her same sex attraction with the words, "And I can't change, even if I tried, even if I wanted to." That is, there is a widespread message in our culture that *same sex attraction equals a gay identity that should be acted on in order to experience fullness of life.* Once we define people by their sexuality, it is easy to see how anything that hinders the expression of their sexuality (ie - "who they really are") becomes a violation of their humanity and personhood.

Christianity wholeheartedly agrees with the human desire to experience fullness of life. But Christianity says this cultural message does not go nearly far enough in empowering people – gay or straight – to experience fullness of life. In fact, our cultural message that attraction equates to identity actually diminishes human dignity because *it reduces a person's core identity to their sexual urges.* Our sexuality is certainly a part of who we are but we are much more than our sexual urges. Reducing people's identity to their sexual urges, whether heterosexual or homosexual, diminishes the greatness of what it means for them to be human.

Our rational ability to choose how we will act on our desires and urges is one thing that separates us from animals. This is why Jonathan Hill writes: "The human being is not a *sexual* being but a choosing being. Our *choices* – for good or evil – with what is given to us *are what we are* before God."[1] In other words, it is not the sexual desires that define who we are, but the choices we make to act on those desires with the bodies we have been given. This is why Hill writes, "anybody's identity as a human being can be defined only by considering how he or she chooses to live."[2]

One may then argue that our identity is about much more than sexual urges; it is also about relationship and love. That is certainly true, but being fully human does not mean that you *have* to be in a romantic relationship. If this were the case, we would need to say that all single people, gay or straight, are not fully human unless they are in a romantic relationship. As wonderful as genuine romantic relationships are, reducing people's identity to the need for a romantic relationship also diminishes the greatness of their humanity. It is very possible to be fully human and to be single, and we do a disservice to single people when we elevate romantic relationships as the standard of what it means to be human.

In summary, we are far more than our sexual urges being expressed in romantic relationships.

OUR VIEW OF HUMANITY IS TOO SMALL

This is the point where God wants to revolutionize how we build our identity. God wants to give all of us, gay or straight, an identity that encompasses all of our humanness, thereby leading to fullness of life.

---

[1] Jonathan Hill, *Love, Covenant & Meaning* (Vancouver: Regent College Publishing, 1997), 34. Emphasis in original.
[2] Hill, *Love, Covenant & Meaning*, 35.

The Bible says our problem is that we have too low a view of what it means to be human. The Bible also declares that we are not merely a random collection of atoms with urges and appetites. Rather, we are the special creation of God himself. We were made to know and be in a relationship with our Creator. The human soul is so great that God alone can sustain the weight of it. This means that trying to build our identity on anything but God is like trying to build a skyscraper on sinking sand. Sand cannot uphold such greatness and the skyscraper will crumble. In the same way, if we try to build our identity on anything but God, the greatness of our humanity will crumble.

We know this is true in other areas of life. If we try to build our identity and self-worth on being physically attractive we will crumble, because we will never be attractive enough and, in the end, age will steal all our youthful beauty from us. If we try to build our identity and self-worth on being successful, we will either become prideful and look down on those who do not achieve as much as we do, or we will always feel like a failure for not achieving anything.

In like manner, if we try to place the full weight of our identity on another person within a romantic relationship we will crush them, because no person can bear the weight of all we want and need.

Into all of this Jesus comes with an astounding promise. In John 10:10 Jesus said, "I have come that you might have life and have it to the full." Jesus is saying that he wants all people, gay or straight, to experience the fullness of what it means to be human. He is saying that he is pro-human and calling us to build our identity on him, for he alone can sustain the weight of all we are. Our culture says same sex attraction equals identity, while God says one's sexual attraction may be part of one's experience but it does not have to define who we are. Therefore, God calls us to build our identity, not on our sexual urges, but on Jesus Christ who made us, who knows us, who came to rescue us, and who will lead us into the fullness of what it means to be human.

AN IDENTITY BEYOND SEXUAL ATTRACTION

Wesley Hill wrote a book entitled *Washed and Waiting*. He states that he has always felt same sex attraction but chooses not to act on this attraction. He does this because he believes his identity is built on Jesus Christ and not on one single part of who he is as a human being.

> …being gay isn't the most important thing about my or any other gay person's identity. I am a Christian before I am anything else. My homosexuality is a part of my makeup, a facet of my personality. One day, I believe, whether in this life or in the resurrection, it will fade away. But my identity as a Christian—someone incorporated into Christ's body by his Spirit—will remain… Imitating Jesus; conforming my thoughts, beliefs, desires, and hopes to his; sharing his life; embracing his gospel's no to homosexual practice—I become more fully alive, not less. According to the Christian story, true Christ-like holiness is the same thing as true humanness. To renounce homosexual behavior [sic] is to say yes to full, rich, abundant life.[3]

Sam Allberry, who has the same experience as Wesley Hill and is also a pastor, writes, "The kind of sexual attractions I experience are not fundamental to my identity. They are part of what I feel but are not who I am in a fundamental sense. I am

---

[3] Wesley Hill, *Washed and Waiting: Reflections on Christian Faithfulness and Homosexuality* (Grand Rapids: Zondervan, 2010), Kindle Edition, Location 146, 869.

far more than my sexuality."[4] This contrasts sharply with those gay people who say their attractions *are* their identity. People like Hill and Allberry, who experience same sex attraction, also have a meaningful place in this discussion. Hill isn't denying his attraction to the same sex. Rather, he and so many others are choosing not to form their identity around their attractions but around Jesus.

Jesus said, "If anyone would come after me, he must deny himself and take up his cross daily and follow me. For whoever wants to save his life will lose it, but whoever loses his life for me and for the gospel will save it."[5] There is no question Jesus asks much from us. He calls everyone, regardless of sexual orientation, to deny our very selves. He calls us to surrender every part of who we are to him and to daily build our identity on him. But the reason we should do this, Jesus says, is because in him is all the fullness of life for which we are searching.

To summarize, God must not be anti-gay. After all, Jesus, God's Son, states that his very reason for coming is that we might have life and have it to the full. In order that we might find fullness of life, God seeks to revolutionize our identity around the one Person who can sustain the weight of our humanness – Jesus Christ.

---

[4] Sam Allberry, *Is God Anti-Gay? And other questions about homosexuality, the Bible and same sex attraction* (Croydon: The Good Book Company, 2013), 8-9.
[5] Mark 8:34-35.

Chapter 3
The God Who Gives Liberating Boundaries

At this point the question may be, "Can people build their identity on Jesus and still live a homosexual lifestyle?" In other words, what are God's rules about sexuality? Someone will then say, "Aha, I knew it. Now we will see the Bible verses that speak against homosexuality. Now we will see that God is indeed anti-gay." Well, let's find out.

FREEDOM WITHIN BOUNDARIES

In our day most people do not like the idea of rules, especially in the area of sexuality. True freedom, they say, means being free to do whatever we like. True freedom means no boundaries. That sounds so good, but we all know it simply isn't true. True freedom is always found within strict boundaries. Musicians are most free, not when they strike any note they happen to hit, but when they stay within the strict rules of music (like playing in the correct key). While driving, you are most free not when you ignore the centre line but when you submit to the very strict rule of driving on the right side of the road (or the left, in some countries). Goldfish are most free, not when they jump out of their fishbowls and onto the counter, but when they heed the boundaries of water and air.

Skydivers are most free to enjoy the exhilaration of free-fall only when they submit to the very strict rules of gravity that require them to open their parachutes at a safe distance from the ground.

The Bible says that God's rules are not arbitrary laws to ruin our fun. They are rather the good instructions of our Creator for how life works best. God's rules on all things (including sexuality) are his good instructions to protect and enhance human flourishing. You might say they are the manufacturer's instructions for the human species. When your car manufacturer says not to put water in your gas tank, the manufacturer is not trying to ruin your freedom. The manufacturer is trying to protect and enhance your freedom. If we can agree that some rules are for our own good, or at least acknowledge that not all rules are bad, then we are prepared to understand God's rules on human sexuality.

GOD'S RULES ON SEXUALITY

It may come as a surprise to some people, but the Bible says sex is God's good gift to humanity. God is not a prude who says, "OK, if you really have to have sex then go ahead but I don't like it." This is not the case at all. We read in Genesis 2 that when God created Adam and Eve he gave sex to them as a gift to express and cement their unity with each other. Since sex so powerfully bonds two people together, God created marriage as the boundary for sexuality. Genesis 2:24 says, "For this reason a man will leave his father and mother and be united to his wife, and they will become one flesh." Jesus himself reinforced this in his teachings on marriage and divorce. So the Bible teaches that sex is God's good gift to be enjoyed between a man and woman within marriage.

When it comes to homosexuality, it may again be a surprise to learn that the Bible is not fixated on it. As Sam Allberry writes, "when it does [speak]…the Bible has important and clear things to say about homosexuality."[1] Let me summarize it like this: The Bible doesn't condemn homosexual *orientation/inclination*, only sexual *lust* or *activity* outside of a marriage relationship between a husband and wife.

For instance, in Leviticus 18, God gives his people rules regarding with whom and what they can and cannot have sex. When people accuse the Bible of being out of touch with modern life, I have to chuckle. Leviticus 18 makes even *The Jerry Springer Show* seem tame by comparison. Even a short course in world history will demonstrate that ancient people were just as – if not even more – interested in exploring every possible way to experience sexual pleasure as we are today. For this reason, Leviticus 18 is a long chapter of sexual prohibitions. God commands his people not to have sex with animals, one's mother, father, sister, brother, son-in-law, daughter-in-law, aunt, uncle, or the wife of one's neighbour. This long list shows that, because we are sinners, our sexual desires can be misdirected in many different ways. We can see that our sexuality is misdirected in our own day, for example, when men objectify women and when spouses cheat on each other. So the question is not, "Is our sexuality misdirected?" but rather "In what ways is our sexuality misdirected?"

It is within this list of over twenty ways that our sexuality is described as being misdirected that we find a reference to homosexual behaviour: "Do not lie with a man as one lies with a woman."[2] Notice that homosexuality is not given a chapter of its own and neither is it singled out for special focus. Contrary to the way it is sometimes presented, homosexuality is listed as

---

[1] Allberry, *Is God Anti-Gay?*, 23.
[2] Leviticus 18:22.

one sexual act among many that is outside God's good intention for humanity.

The rest of the Bible follows the same track. Romans chapter 1, for instance, describes a long list of behaviours that demonstrate how people have turned away from God. This list includes envy, strife, deceit, malice, gossip, slander, and pride. Within this discussion the author Paul writes, "...women exchanged natural relations for unnatural ones. In the same way the men also abandoned natural relations with women and were inflamed with lust for one another. Men committed indecent acts with other men..."[3]

TO DISAGREE IS NOT TO HATE

But someone will say, "If God is clearly against people acting on same sex attraction, then God must be anti-gay." I submit that we only think this way because our culture always forces people into only one of two viewpoints. Our culture says we either celebrate homosexuality (and are therefore viewed as loving and tolerant toward gay people) or we disagree with homosexuality (and are therefore viewed as being against gay people, homophobic, bigoted, and anti-gay). For instance, I saw

---

[3] Romans 1:26-27. Although the Christian Church has historically and universally understood these and other texts to forbid homosexual behaviour, many recent authors have called this interpretation into question. Generally speaking these recent authors have argued that the Bible, when read in its historical context, does not condemn committed, consensual, monogamous, same-sex unions but only exploitative or excessive homosexual behaviour such as homosexual gang rape (Gen 19), homosexual cult prostitution (Lev 18:22), hedonistic forms of homosexuality (Rom 1), and homosexual pedophilia (I Cor 6:8; I Tim 1:10). Although a detailed review of this new perspective is outside the scope of these short chapters, I recommend those wanting to study the biblical texts to read: Gagnon, Robert. *The Bible And Homosexual Practice: Texts And Hermeneutics*. Nashville: Abington Press, 2010.

---

one promotional image that said, "The issue of gay marriage is simple. Choose one." Underneath were two options. The first said, "I'm for equality" and the second said, "I'm a bigot."

Perhaps, however, there is another way to view this issue – a third way that is often missed. Is it possible to disagree with someone and yet still love them? Of course it is possible. *To disagree is not to hate* – at least it does not have to mean this.[4] Many people disagree with Christianity but it does not necessarily follow that they hate Christians, are Christophobic, or anti-Christian. In many areas of life it is very possible to say, "I believe you are wrong, but I love you nevertheless." Embracing this kind of tolerance will go a long way to developing a society where all people, regardless of religious beliefs and even sexual orientation, are treated with respect.

In summary, God gives boundaries for our sexuality, not because he is anti-gay, but because he is our Creator who loves us and knows how we function best. God's rules for sexuality are designed to protect and enhance human flourishing. When God disagrees with our choice to pursue same sex relationships or to live promiscuously, it does not mean God is either anti-gay or anti-sex. To disagree is not to hate.

Despite all that has been said above, many people may still feel that God is anti-gay. In the next chapter I will reveal the Bible's ultimate proof that God is not against gay people.

---

[4] The first part of this sentence is inspired by Trevin Wax, "How I wish the homosexuality debate would go," The Gospel Coalition, entry posted October 18, 2011, http://www.thegospelcoalition.org/blogs/trevinwax /2011/10/18/ how-i-wish-the-homosexuality-debate-would-go/ (accessed Apr 10, 2015). Wax says, "to differ is not to hate."

Chapter 4
The God Who Loves Sacrificially

The supreme proof that God is not against gay people is found in the story of Jesus Christ. At the very heart of this story is self-sacrifice. Christianity teaches that all human beings are separated from God because of our sin. However, out of love, God became a man in order to remove our sin and reconcile us to himself. He did this by voluntarily sacrificing his own life on the cross. The message of Christianity is that Jesus took upon himself the punishment and death that we deserve for our sin. He died the death that we should have died in order that we might be reconciled to God and live with him forever.

SELF-SACRIFICE CANNOT BE HATRED

In our culture we have countless stories of one person sacrificing his or her life for another. In literature we see this theme in Charles Dickens's *A Tale of Two Cities*. Charles Darnay and Sydney Carton both love the same woman named Lucie Manett, but Lucie chooses to marry Charles and Sydney is left alone. Later in the story, Charles is thrown into prison where he awaits execution by guillotine. Sydney visits him in prison, drugs him, and has him carried out. Sydney then secretly takes Charles' place at the guillotine. He sacrifices his life so that his opponent, Charles, can live happily ever after.

The theme of self-sacrifice comes up again and again in our movies. In *The Lion the Witch and the Wardrobe*, Aslan allows himself to be killed by the White Witch so that Edmund can avoid the death penalty. In *The Matrix*, Neo gives his life so the human race can be freed from the machines. In *Titanic*, Jack voluntarily freezes to death in the frigid waters so Rose can stay afloat and eventually be rescued. In *Frozen*, princess Anna sacrificially gives her life for her sister Elsa. The *Harry Potter* series ends when Harry sacrifices himself in death only to come back to life and defeat the evil Lord Voldemort. In *The Lord of the Rings* Gandalf sacrifices himself on the bridge of Khazad-dum to ensure that his friends escape. These stories move us because it is the supreme example of love when one gives up his or her life for another, especially if that person is an adversary. No one who sacrifices his or her own life for another can be accused of hatred.

The apostle Paul summarizes the message of Christianity in his letter to the Romans. He writes, "Very rarely will anyone die for a righteous man, though for a good man someone might possibly dare to die. But God demonstrates his own love for us in this: While we were still sinners, Christ died for us... when we were God's enemies, we were reconciled to him through the death of his Son."[1] You see, the entire message of Christianity is that, despite our sins, God has not rejected us. Rather, God sent his only Son to die in our place that we might be forgiven, reconciled to him, and given an eternity of joy in his presence. How can we think God is anti-gay when, out of love, God gave us Jesus who willingly died for the sins of people, gay or

---

[1] Romans 5:7-8, 10.

straight? The cross proves that, if we think God is anti-gay, we have been led astray in our thinking. In sacrificing himself, Jesus indisputably proved his love for all sinners, regardless of their sexual orientation.

PUTTING IT ALL TOGETHER

Is God anti-gay? These four chapters on *Homosexuality & God* have argued that God is not anti-gay. First, they state that he is the radically inclusive God who created all people (gay or straight) in his image and therefore demands that all people (regardless of sexual orientation) be treated with dignity, value, and respect. God's radical inclusivity is also seen in the fact that he sent his Son to rescue all types of sinners that "whoever believes in him will not perish but have eternal life."[2]

The second piece of evidence that God is not anti-gay stated that his purpose in sending Jesus to this world was that we might have "life and have it to the full."[3] God cares so much about the core identity of people, gay or straight, that he seeks to revolutionize our identity around Jesus Christ who is the one person who can sustain the greatness of who we are as human beings.

Third, when God's rules seem to contradict our sexual practices, it does not mean God is anti-gay, for to disagree is not to hate. God gives liberating boundaries for our sexuality, not because he is anti-gay, but because he is our Creator who made us and therefore knows how we function best.

Finally, the ultimate proof that God is not anti-gay is found in the fact that God became a man and sacrificed himself for us in

---

[2] John 3:16b.
[3] John 10:10.

order that we might be reconciled to him. A person cannot be accused of hate when he or she sacrifices his or her own life for another.

After reading these chapters on *Homosexuality & God* it is my hope that non-Christians, who have previously rejected Christianity because of a perceived anti-gay bias, can feel that this obstacle need no longer inhibit their being open to consider the claims of Jesus Christ. Additionally, it is my hope that Christians who have rejected or even expressed hostility toward gay people will turn away from such attitudes and demonstrate genuine love. I also hope that those who feel same-sex attraction will discover a God who made them in his image, who offers a lasting identity that leads to fullness of life; a God who sacrificed himself that "whoever believes him will not perish but have eternal life."

PROBLEM #2:
MIRACLES & SCIENCE

WHY SHOULD I BELIEVE IN MIRACLES
IN AN AGE OF SCIENCE?

INTRODUCTION

Christianity rises or falls on whether or not certain miracles actually took place. The greatest example of this is the miracle of Jesus' resurrection. In 1 Corinthians 15:17 the apostle Paul writes, "if Christ has not been raised, your faith is futile; you are still in your sins." In other words, the historical fact of Jesus' resurrection is so foundational to Christianity that, if it is proved to be false, the Christian faith would collapse.

Many say that the problem with Christianity is its emphasis on miracles. How can anyone with even a high school level of education and living in the 21st century believe that a virgin conceived a child, a man walked on water, or a corpse rose from the dead? The 18th century philosopher David Hume, who wrote arguably the most famous book against the existence of miracles, remarked that belief in miracles is most often found among "ignorant and barbarous nations."[1] The obvious implication of such a statement is that educated and civilized people know better than to believe in miracles.

There is no question that the scientific advances of even the last one hundred years are nothing short of astounding. We have eradicated small pox and developed antibiotics, walked on the moon, split the atom, replaced the horse with the car, the typewriter with the computer, the radio with the Internet, and the telegraph with the smartphone. In view of this small sampling of scientific advancement, how can civilized and educated people still believe in miracles? Even in the mid part of the 20th century, the German professor Rudolf Bultmann said, "It is impossible to use electric light and the wireless and to avail ourselves of modern medical and surgical discoveries,

---

[1] David Hume, "Of Miracles" in *An Inquiry Concerning Human Understanding*, ed. Charles W. Hendel (Indianapolis: Boobs-Merrill Co., 1955), 126.

and at the same time to believe in the New Testament world of spirits and miracles."[2] Along the same lines, but more current, is the statement of Richard Dawkins: "Any belief in miracles is flatly contradictory not just to the facts of science but also to the spirit of science."[3]

Since those of us in the western world have grown up breathing the air of "science-has-disproved-miracles and only-gullible-people-believe-in-miracles", we commonly come to this issue with a collection of biases that keep us from believing in miracles and thus embracing Christianity. In the next few chapters I will identify and critically examine four of these collective biases giving particular attention to the miraculous claim of Jesus' resurrection. I will ask you to consider our bias against the supernatural (chapter 5); our bias toward scientism (chapter 6); our bias against ancient people (chapters 7-8); and our bias against God himself (chapter 9).

---

[2] Rudolf Bultmann, *Kerygma And Myth* (New York: Harper, 1961), 4-5.
[3] Dawkins quotes in David Van Biema, "God vs. Science", *Time*, November 5, 2006. http://content.time.com/time/magazine/article/ 0,9171,155513 2-3,00. html (accessed Apr 10, 2015).

Chapter 5
Our Bias Against The Supernatural

[He is the type of man who] will always find in himself the strength and ability not to believe in miracles...and if a miracle stands before him as an irrefutable fact, he will sooner doubt his own senses than admit the fact. And if he does admit it, he will admit it as a fact of nature that was previously unknown to him.[1]

- Fyodor Dostoevsky's description of a
character in *The Brothers Karamazov*

A bias against the supernatural is at the very foundation of why people believe miracles are impossible. Indeed, the whole question of miracles comes down to whether you are a naturalist or a supernaturalist.[2]

---

[1] Fyodor Dostoevsky, *The Brothers Karamazov*, trans Richard Pevear and Larissa Volokhonsky, (New York: Everyman's Library Alfred A. Knopf Publishing, 1990), 25-26.

[2] For the subsequent discussion on naturalism and supernaturalism see Ronald Nash, *Life's Ultimate Questions: An Introduction to Philosophy* (Grand Rapids: Zondervan, 1999), 38.

UNDERSTANDING NATURALISM

To understand naturalism, imagine a closed box that is sealed at every corner. Inside the box is everything that exists in the natural order that we call the universe. Furthermore, there is nothing outside the box; no God and no supernatural realm. Carl Sagan sums up naturalism with his trademark slogan, "The Cosmos is all there is or ever was or ever will be." Naturalism, then, is the belief that the natural universe is the sum total of reality.

Miracles are impossible to a naturalist because 1) there is nothing outside the universe that can have an effect within the universe 2) everything that happens in the universe can be explained in terms of natural causes. The naturalist, therefore, argues that we do not need to resort to miracles or magic to explain events that seem mysterious to us because, ultimately, there is a natural explanation for everything that happens. There is not much point in trying to convince a naturalist that there is such thing as miracles because he or she has already decided that they are impossible. If confronted by a true miracle the naturalist would explain it away by saying, "My senses must have deceived me", or "I don't have an explanation but I assume there is a scientific explanation that does not involve the miraculous."

UNDERSTANDING SUPERNATURALISM

Supernaturalism also begins by imagining a box that contains the whole natural order of the universe. However, in this image there is something that exists both within and outside the box, namely, God. In Christian teaching, God created the box and everything in it: "In the beginning God created the heavens and the earth."[3] God did not create the heavens and the earth from pre-existing matter; he created everything in the box *ex nihilo* (out of nothing): "...the universe was formed at God's command, so that what is seen was not made out of what was visible."[4] Furthermore, Christianity teaches that, although God exists within the box, he also transcends it and is therefore not limited to the life inside the box. Supernaturalism, then, is the belief that there is a supernatural reality that exists within and beyond the natural universe.

Christianity teaches that God acts within the universe in at least two ways. First, God acts within the box to uphold and sustain all that he created. God did not just create natural laws, like gravity, and then leave the universe to run except when he wants to re-enter the box to work a miracle. Rather, Christianity teaches that Jesus, the Son of God, also continues to sustain what he created: "The Son is the radiance of God's glory and the exact representation of his being, *sustaining all things by his powerful word.*"[5] In this sense God is always at work within his universe so that the Bible can describe rain as coming from the clouds and as coming from God himself.[6] If he did not so act, all things would cease to exist. This means that while Christians in the past sometimes erred in labeling things as miraculous that could be explained in natural terms, they were not entirely wrong, for the Bible teaches that God is ultimately behind all things.

Second, Christianity teaches that God occasionally acts in ways that cannot be explained by natural causes. Miracles are

---

[3] Genesis 1:1.

[4] Hebrews 11:3.

[5] Hebrews 1:3.

[6] For instance, compare Ecclesiastes 3:11: "If clouds are full of water, they pour rain upon the earth", with Psalm 147:7-8: "Sing to the Lord with thanksgiving; make music to our God on the harp. He covers the sky with clouds; he supplies the earth with rain."

possible within supernaturalism because God exists outside the universe and yet is able to act within it. This is why the Bible teaches that the "Lord God Almighty reigns", that nothing is too hard for God, that "with God all things are possible," and that "he does whatever pleases him."[7]

But why would God so act? The Bible teaches that God has done so in order to reveal himself to his creatures. T.F. Torrance writes,

> If God really is God, the Creator of all things visible and invisible and the Source of all rational order in the universe, I find it absurd to think that he does not actively reveal himself to us but remains inert and aloof, so that we are left to grope about in the dark for possible intimations and clues to his reality.[8]

Bruce Milne further develops this thought by adding that it is perfectly reasonable to believe a loving God would reveal himself:

> If we supposed, further, as many do, even vaguely, that the Creator God is loving, the likelihood of revelation becomes overwhelming; what loving parent would deliberately keep out of a child's sight and range of reference so that it grew up ignorant of its parent's existence?

THE DEBATE IS NOT REALLY ABOUT MIRACLES

In light of this entire discussion on naturalism and supernaturalism, you can see that the debate about miracles is not actually a debate about miracles at all; it is actually a debate about the existence of God and the kind of God he is if he *does*

---

[7] Revelation 19:6; Genesis 18:14; Matthew 19:26; Psalm 115:3.
[8] Bruce Milne, *Know the Truth: A handbook of Christian belief,* 3rd ed. (Nottingham: Intervarsity Press, 2009), 27.

exist. If you say miracles are impossible, then you must realize that you are making a much bigger claim than the mere impossibility of specific events like Jesus healing a man from leprosy. You are actually claiming to know with total certainty that God does not exist. After all, if God exists it would not be difficult for him to walk on water or to part the waters of the Red Sea. If God exists and can create the universe, then surely he could turn water to wine, make a blind man see, or raise someone from the dead. Therefore, to deny the existence of miracles you must have an airtight case against the existence of God, because if God exists, miracles are perfectly possible and plausible.

In this chapter I am not trying to prove the existence of God – my goal is far more modest. I am simply asking you to consider that any claim against the existence of miracles is actually a claim against the existence of God. Can anyone make such an enormous claim? Can anyone prove beyond all doubt that God does not exist? If not, then I am asking you to consider, at the very least, that miracles are possible. Admittedly this does not prove the truth of any miraculous claim, but it does show that our difficulty with miracles arises not from scientific facts, but from a bias against the supernatural; a bias that assumes, but cannot prove, that God does not exist.

Chapter 6
Our Bias Toward Scientism

The existence of a limit to science is, however, made clear by its inability to answer childlike elementary questions having to do with first and last things – questions such as: "How did everything begin?" "What are we all here for?" "What is the point of living?" [1]

- Nobel Laureate Sir Peter Medawar

SCIENCE VS. SCIENTISM

A bias toward scientism is not the same thing as a bias toward science. The Christian faith has no conflict with science (understood as a discipline that seeks to discover and explain how the universe works). Christianity teaches that God is a rational being and therefore rational laws, not chaos or irrationality, govern his creation. Further, since God gave human beings the ability to reason, it is possible for us to use our powers of observation to discover the secrets of the

---

[1] Peter Medawar, *Advice to a Young Scientist*, (London: Harper and Row, 1979), 31. For almost the same wording see also Peter Medawar, *The Limits of Science* (Oxford: Oxford University Press, 1984), 66.

universe. To the Christian, science is rational (for the universe reflects its rational Creator) and useful (for in discovering God's universe we are discovering God himself). In the words of Johannes Kepler, "The chief aim of all investigations of the external world should be to discover the rational order and harmony imposed on it by God and which he revealed to us in the language of mathematics."[2] In like manner, the great chemist, Robert Boyle, wrote to the Royal Society of London, wishing them continued success in "their laudable attempts to discover the true Nature of the Works of God."[3]

Science seeks to understand and explain the universe but scientism goes much further. Scientism is the belief that science has no limits and that "science is the only way to truth and it can, at least in principle, explain everything."[4] Dr. Peter Atkins, the atheist and former professor of chemistry at Oxford, described scientism when he wrote, "There is no reason to suppose that science cannot deal with every aspect of existence."[5] Bertrand Russell, the philosopher and mathematician, asserts the same thing: "Whatever knowledge is

---

[2] Cited in Rodney Stark, *The Triumph of Christianity: How the Jesus movement became the world's largest religion* (New York: HarperOne, 2011), 287.

[3] Rodney Stark, *The Triumph of Christianity*, 287. This view was shared by Francis Bacon (1561-1626), who is regarded to be the father of modern science. He spoke of the two books of God – the book of Nature and the Bible – and that people should give attention to studying both. Many other great figures of science were also theists and Christians. They were convinced that belief in God, far from hindering science, gave the inspiration for it. This includes such men as Galileo (1564-1642), Kepler (1571-1630), Pascal (1623-62), Boyle (1627-91), Newton (1642-1727), Faraday (1791-1867), Babbage (1791-1871), Mendel (1822-84), Pasteur (1822-95), Kelvin (1824-1907) and Clerk Maxwell (1831-79). For more on this, see John Lennox, *God's Undertaker: Has Science Buried God?* (Oxford: A Lion Book, 2009), 18-22.

[4] John Lennox, *God's Undertaker: Has Science Buried God?* (Oxford: A Lion Book, 2009), Kindle Edition Location 802.

[5] Peter Atkins, *Nature's Imagination: the Frontiers of Scientific Vision*, ed. John Cornwell (Oxford: Oxford University Press, 1995), 125.

attainable, must be attained by scientific methods; and what science cannot discover, mankind cannot know."[6] The thoughts of Atkins and Russell are echoed in a conversation I once had with a university student at a local pub. Before the nachos and hot wings even arrived, he asserted his primary objection to Christianity saying, "Why should I believe in God when science can explain everything?"

When people move from science to scientism they also move from being open to the possibility of miracles to believing that they are impossible, for scientism excludes as unscientific all talk about God and miracles. Here again we see that there is not much point in trying to prove the existence of miracles to one who embraces scientism because he or she has decided beforehand that miracles are impossible. Rather, we must challenge the presupposed bias that science has the ability to explain everything. If it can be shown that science is limited in its ability to explain reality, then miracles may exist outside the realm of what science can address. In this chapter I want to challenge our bias toward scientism by showing the limitations of science in two specific areas.

SCIENCE CANNOT ANSWER OUR MOST BASIC QUESTIONS

First, science is limited in that it cannot answer some of our most basic and important questions about life. Dr. John Lennox, professor of mathematics at the University of Oxford, illustrates this by asking us to imagine that his Aunt Matilda has baked a beautiful cake. Along with Lennox we take the cake to a group of the world's top scientists and ask them to explain it. Since they are great scientists we can learn a great deal from

---

[6] Bertrand Russell, *Religion and Science* (Oxford: Oxford University Press, 1970), 243.

them. The nutritionists tell us the nutritional information such as how many calories are in the cake. The biochemists tell us about all the proteins and fats. The chemists teach us about the elements in the cake and how they bond. The physicists even analyze the cake's fundamental particles.

Once we have all this data can we say the cake has been fully explained? Not really. We know a great deal about the cake, but there is one big question that lingers: why did Aunt Matilda make the cake? We look at her and can see there is a big grin on her face; she knows why she baked it. All the scientists in the world cannot answer that question. This is not to say they are bad scientists or that science is useless. It is simply to say that science can only go so far. Science can answer some of the "how" questions but it cannot answer the "why" questions that concern the purpose of the cake. Aunt Matilda must reveal the answer to us and no amount of scientific analysis will solve the riddle.[7]

This is why Nobel Laureate Sir Peter Medawar writes in his book *Advice to a Young Scientist*:

> There is no quicker way for a scientist to bring discredit upon himself and upon his profession than roundly to declare…that science knows, or soon will know, the answers to all questions worth asking…The existence of a limit to science is, however, made clear by its inability to answer childlike elementary questions having to do with first and last things – questions such as: "How did everything begin?" "What are we all here for?" "What is the point of living?"[8]

Francis Collins, Director of the Human Genome Project, agrees: "Science is powerless to answer questions such as 'Why

---

[7] Lennox, *God's Undertaker*, Location 833.
[8] Medawar, *Advice to a Young Scientist*, 31.

did the universe come into being?' 'What is the meaning of human existence?' 'What happens after we die?'"[9] These scientists are not trying to devalue scientific discovery or science itself. To the contrary, they are simply asking us to consider our bias toward scientism; to recognize that there are areas to which science cannot speak. Ironically, these types of questions that science cannot answer are the ones that matter most to us as human beings.

If science is the only true source of knowledge, as Russell asserts, then universities need to get rid of all ethics classes (for science cannot define what is right and wrong), art classes (for science cannot tell us what is beautiful), law classes (for science cannot tell us what makes a law just), philosophy classes (for science cannot answer metaphysical questions), literature classes (for science cannot tell us what makes a great novel or poem), and music classes (for science cannot tell us if Mozart is better or worse than Katy Perry). Science can tell us many things, but it is limited in that it cannot answer some of our most basic and important questions about life.

SCIENCE CANNOT PROVE
OR DISPROVE GOD'S EXISTENCE

Second, science is limited in that it cannot prove or disprove the existence of God. To be fair, Christians cannot empirically prove or disprove God's existence either. But this is precisely the point; namely, that God is beyond the reach of scientific discovery because he is above and beyond the natural order in

---

[9] Cited in Lennox, *God's Undertaker*, Location 857.

which the scientific method operates.[10] There is no telescope or microscope that can see God and no instrument that can measure him. Therefore, the question of God's existence, and thus of miracles, is not one that can be ultimately decided by science. Christianity asserts, rather, that scientific discovery should *point* us to the existence of God "for since the creation of the world God's invisible qualities—his eternal power and divine nature—have been clearly seen, being understood from what has been made, so that men are without excuse." [11] But this is different from saying the existence of God can be *proved* through the scientific method.

Reflecting this limitation of science to prove or disprove God's existence, the *U.S. National Academy of Sciences* states, "Science is a way of knowing about the natural world. It is limited to explaining the natural world through natural causes. Science can say nothing about the supernatural. Whether God exists or not is a question about which science is neutral."[12] Stephen Gould, the Harvard paleontologist and committed atheist, concurs: "To say it for my colleagues and for the umpteenth millionth time…science simply cannot (by its legitimate methods) adjudicate the issue of God's possible superintendence of nature. We neither affirm nor deny it; we simply can't comment on it as scientists."[13]

---

[10] Definition of scientific method: "principles and procedures for the systematic pursuit of knowledge involving the recognition and formulation of a problem, the collection of data through observation and experiment, and the formulation and testing of hypotheses." Merriam-Webster Dictionary. http://www.merriam-webster.com/dictionary/scientific %20method (accessed April 10, 2015).

[11] Romans 1:20.

[12] Victor J. Stenger, *God: The Failed Hypothesis – How Science Shows That God Does Not Exist* (Amherst: Prometheus Books, 2008), 28.

[13] Richard Dawkins, *The God Delusion* (Boston: Houghton Mifflin Company, 2008), 78.

SCIENTIFIC EVIDENCE FOR GOD

For centuries many of the greatest scientists and philosophers have been pointing out that, while science cannot prove or disprove God's existence, it does provide solid evidence that points toward the existence of God. This evidence has led many to change their minds about the existence of God. Perhaps one of the most astonishing examples of this is the English philosopher, Antony Flew. For most of his life, Flew was a powerful advocate of atheism. He was sharply critical of religion and signed the *Humanist Manifesto* in 2003. However, in 2004, at the age of 81, Flew changed his views stating that he was simply following his lifelong commitment to go wherever the evidence led him. To give an account of the arguments and evidence that led him to this he wrote a book entitled, *There is a God: How the World's Most Notorious Atheist Changed His Mind*. Flew argues that, while science cannot prove or disprove God, it does provide at least three pieces of evidence that cannot be explained apart from God:

> Science qua science cannot furnish an argument for God's existence. But the three items of evidence we have considered in this volume—the laws of nature, life with its teleological organization, and the existence of the universe—can only be explained in the light of an Intelligence that explains both its own existence and that of the world. Such a discovery of the Divine does not come through experiments and equations, but through an understanding of the structures they unveil and map.[14]

As Flew works through these pieces of evidence he often cites Albert Einstein. Some have claimed Einstein was an atheist, but

---

[14] Antony Flew, *There is a God: How the World's Most Notorious Atheist Changed His Mind* (New York: HarperCollins e-books, 2007), Kindle Edition, Location 1702.

Einstein himself categorically denied this. Although not a Christian, Einstein also believed that the scientific evidence on the laws of nature points to the existence of God. Flew quotes Einstein:

> I'm not an atheist, and I don't think I can call myself a pantheist. We are in the position of a little child entering a huge library filled with books in many languages. The child knows someone must have written those books. It does not know how. It does not understand the languages in which they are written. The child dimly suspects a mysterious order in the arrangement of the books but doesn't know what it is. *That, it seems to me, is the attitude of even the most intelligent human being toward God. We see the universe marvelously arranged and obeying certain laws but only dimly understand these laws. Our limited minds grasp the mysterious force that moves the constellations.*[15]

Stephen Meyer elaborates by citing further examples of how science affirms, and points to, the existence of God.[16]

- Current Big Bang theory and its accompanying theoretical foundation in general relativity point to a definitive beginning to the universe. Yet, if the universe had a beginning, we cannot invoke time, matter, energy, or the laws of nature to explain where it came from. General relativity requires a cause outside of these things in order for them to exist.

- The fundamental laws and parameters of physics have to possess precise numerical values. If this is not the case then our universe does not exist as it does. For

---

[15] Flew, *There is a God*, Location 1184. Emphasis mine.
[16] The following bullet points paraphrased from Lee Strobel, *The Case for the Creator: A Journalist Investigates Scientific Evidence That Points Toward God* (Grand Rapids: Zondervan, 2004), 77-82.

instance, if the universe, which is fine-tuned to one part in a trillion trillion trillion trillion trillion were changed by even a single part – either faster or slower – our universe could not support life.

- The information that is required to form life (stored in DNA and protein molecules) points to a Creator. Every experience we have about information from computers, to books, to cave drawings points toward an intelligent designer.

- Certain biological organisms give evidence of what Michael Behe calls "irreducible complexity." They require all of their various parts in order to function and therefore could not have evolved through natural selection acting on random variations. It is impossible, in evolutionary theory, for an organism to make a giant leap forward through mere chance to create the entire system at once.

- The physical matter in the brain cannot account for human consciousness that has the capacity for self-reflection, art, language, and creativity. "Only the existence of a transcendent Mind explains the effective operation of our human intelligence."[17] In the words of Marvin Minsky, we are not just a "computer made of meat." Roy Abraham Varghese asks us to think about a marble table. "Do you think that given a trillion years, or infinite time, this table could suddenly or gradually become conscious, aware of its surroundings, aware of its identity the way you are? It is simply inconceivable...and what holds for the table holds for all the other matter in the universe."[18]

---

[17] Milne, *Know the Truth*, 73.
[18] Milne, *Know the Truth*, 73.

SUMMARY

In this chapter I am trying to enable you to critique the collective bias toward scientism because this bias causes one to reject miracles before even considering them. Although science can teach us a tremendous number of facts, it is limited in what it can speak to as evidence by the fact that it cannot answer some of the basic "why" questions of our existence. Furthermore, since science is limited in what it can say about the existence or non-existence of God, it is also limited in its ability to discuss miracles.

Chapter 7
Our Bias Against Ancient People (Part 1)

One must state it plainly. Religion comes from the period of human prehistory where nobody…had the smallest idea what was going on. It comes from the bawling and fearful infancy of our species, and is a babyish attempt to meet our inescapable demand for knowledge (as well as for comfort, reassurance, and other infantile needs).[1]

- Christopher Hitchens

In dark ages people are best guided by religion, as in a pitch black night a blind man is the best guide; he knows the roads and paths better than the man who can see. When daylight comes, however, it is foolish to use blind old men as guides.[2]

- 19th century German poet Heinrich Hein

It is common to hear people say, "I am sure that Christianity once seemed reasonable but times have changed. When ancient people heard miracle stories, like Jesus rising from the dead, they were inclined to believe them because such stories

---

[1] Christopher Hitchens, *god Is Not Great: How Religion Poisons Everything* (Toronto: McClelland & Stewart, 2007), 64.
[2] Hitchens, *god Is Not Great*, 43.

resonated with their uneducated, uncivilized, and superstitious worldviews. We in the modern world know better." This is what David Hume was getting at when he declared that people who believe in miracles are most often found among "ignorant and barbarous nations."[3] The trouble with this view of ancient people is that it is simply not true.

Within the Bible itself there are many stories of pre-scientific people who were highly skeptical of miracles. For instance, Joseph did not believe his fiancé Mary when she told him that she was pregnant by the power of the Holy Spirit. During their engagement (which in those days was as legally binding as marriage), Mary had been living away from home for three months with her relative Elizabeth. We can imagine Joseph thinking, "Pregnant by the Holy Spirit? Now I really have heard it all. Is 'Holy Spirit' code for the guy you slept with in Elizabeth's village?" Although not a trained gynecologist, Joseph knew how babies are conceived. Far from believing her story, Joseph decided to divorce her, but to do so quietly in order to save her from the inevitable shame she would face for being labeled an adulteress. Likewise, when Abraham's wife Sarah was told she would have a baby, though "she was past the age of childbearing", she "laughed to herself as she thought, 'After I am worn out and my master is old, will I now have this pleasure?'"[4]

In this chapter I will focus on the resurrection of Jesus and demonstrate that ancient people found such a claim perhaps even more inconceivable than we do today.

In his massive 800-page book, *The Resurrection of the Son of God*, scholar N.T. Wright takes the reader through an exhaustive survey of what people from 200 B.C. to 200 A.D. thought

---

[3] Hume, *An Inquiry Concerning Human Understanding*, 126.
[4] Genesis 18:11-12.

---

about death and the afterlife. Wright shows there were two primary worldviews during this era that reveal what the people of those days thought about the idea of resurrection.

GRECO-ROMAN VIEW OF RESURRECTION

First, the Greco-Roman worldview was very diverse in what it believed happened after death. Just like today, some believed that people cease to exist at death. Also, like today, most believed a person lived as a spirit in another world. These people, however, agreed on one thing: people who die do not come back to life in their bodies. One ancient writer summarizes this universally held conviction: "Once a man has died, and the dust has soaked up his blood, there is no resurrection."[5] Resurrection was an idea that was ridiculed, especially among the educated.

Furthermore, those with a Greco-Roman worldview did not even want resurrection to occur. Most people followed Plato, who taught that what really matters is the soul, not the body. In Platonic thinking, the material world and the body are defiling and corrupt. The body is a prison house for the true self, which is the soul. Death, therefore was viewed as being the soul's liberation from what imprisoned it: "In this worldview resurrection was not only impossible, but totally undesirable. No soul, having gotten free from its body, would ever want it back."[6] We can see that, far from being inclined to believe Jesus rose from the dead, Greco-Roman people thought the very idea of bodily resurrection was impossible, undesirable, and absurd.

---

[5] N.T. Wright, *The Resurrection of the Son of God* (Minneapolis: Fortress Press, 2003), 32.

[6] Timothy Keller, *The Reason for God* (New York: Dutton, 2008), 206.

JEWISH VIEW OF RESURRECTION

Second, the Jewish worldview could not accept the claim that Jesus rose from the dead either, though for different reasons. Jews believed that when God's kingdom came to the earth it would rid the world of things like suffering, death, injustice, and disease. Jews believed that God would corporately resurrect all his people on that great day. Jewish people, then, did not believe that people would ever be resurrected on an individual basis. Wright says, "Nobody imagined that any individuals had already been raised, or would be raised in advance of the great last day."[7] If you walked up to a Jewish man and started telling him that the crucified Rabbi named Jesus had been resurrected, he would say, "Are you insane? How could that be? Look around you. Have disease and death ended? Is true justice established in the world? Obviously not! Therefore the resurrection has not yet happened and your claim is false."[8]

Even those who encountered Jesus after his resurrection had serious doubts. Mary Magdalene was so disinclined to believe in such a miracle that when "she turned around and saw Jesus standing there, but she did not realize that it was Jesus."[9] Matthew tells us that "some doubted" when Jesus appeared to his disciples and gave the Great Commission to "make disciples of all nations."[10] When the message of a risen Jesus was taken out to the ancient world, it was often met with great antagonism. While in Athens, the intellectual centre of the

---

[7] Wright, *The Resurrection of the Son of God*, 205.
[8] Some of this explanation paraphrases Timothy Keller who also borrows from N.T. Wright. See Keller, *The Reason for God*, 201-207.
[9] John 20:14.
[10] Matthew 28:19, 17.

48

ancient world, Paul spoke about the resurrection of Jesus and "some mocked."[11]

ANCIENT PEOPLE WERE SKEPTICS TOO

It is inaccurate, therefore, to say ancient people were more predisposed to believe miracle stories than we are today. Similar to our day, many ancient people were superstitious and quick to believe in the reality of magic and miracles (think about how many people in our culture believe the stars control their destiny, make decisions based on their horoscopes, hang dream catchers in their windows, knock on wood to avoid bad luck, or put crystals in their houses to direct an invisible life force called "qi"). Also similar to our day, many ancient people were highly skeptical about miraculous claims.

As twenty-first century people, we cannot write off the miraculous story of Jesus' resurrection because we think first century people were grossly ignorant, prone to believe such things, while we are more enlightened. First century people found the claim of Jesus' resurrection just as inconceivable as you and I do today, and yet many believed. What overcame their skepticism? This is the subject of the next chapter.

---

[11]Acts 17:32.

Chapter 8
Our Bias Against Ancient People (Part 2)

We still use his name to describe doubt because he was the prototypical ancient skeptic. His name was Thomas; two thousand years later we still call him, "doubting Thomas." He received this name because, like the rest of the ancient world, Thomas was extremely reluctant to believe the story that Jesus had risen from the dead. Yet the Bible tells us that Thomas claimed to have encountered the resurrected Jesus in such a powerful way that one experience removed his doubts, shattered his worldview, and transformed his bias against the possibility of Jesus' resurrection.

The apostle John records the story of Thomas in John chapter 20. John is unapologetic in saying that he recounts this story in order that we too may believe in the miracle of Jesus' resurrection and thus in Jesus himself as God's chosen one, the Son of God. Whether you end up believing Thomas's story or not, this chapter aims to further show that even ancient people (and one of Jesus' own followers in particular) were not inclined to believe the miraculous claim of Jesus rising from the dead.[1]

THE TYPE OF PERSON THOMAS WAS

In recording Thomas' story, John is asking us to consider at least two things. First, we are invited to consider what type of person Thomas was.

> Now Thomas (called Didymus), one of the Twelve, was not with the disciples when Jesus came. So the other disciples told him, "We have seen the Lord!" But he said to them, "Unless I see the nail marks in his hands and put my finger where the nails were, and put my hand into his side, I will not believe it."[2]

Thomas simply could not believe the other disciples' claim that Jesus had risen from the dead. Thomas likely thought, "How gullible do you think I am? There has to be some kind of rational explanation." Thomas is the kind of person who refuses to be taken in by a scam, trick, con, or wishful thinking. You can appreciate Thomas's skepticism, because the world is filled with stories of people, particularly religious ones, being deceived by swindlers.

In the 1980's a man named Peter Popoff had a very large healing ministry. His website reflects on the history of his ministry: "Tens of thousands have been saved, healed, and delivered from every form of demon oppression as the man of God preached the glories of Christ to them. In many countries

---

[1] My discussion on John 20:24-31 borrows from D.A. Carson, *Scandalous: The Cross and Resurrection of Jesus* (Wheaton: Crossway, 2010), 143-168.
[2] John 20:24-25.

people walked for miles to receive supernatural touch through this man's ministry."[3]

At his meetings, Popoff would call out to the audience statements like, "God is giving me a name. Josephine Parino. You have cancer of the stomach. Come down and be healed." Sure enough, Josephine was at the meeting and she did have cancer. Many times Popoff would even call out a name with an exact street address. It all seemed to be clear evidence of the miraculous power of God.

When the world famous magician James Randi and his assistant Steve Shaw were in attendance, they noticed Popoff was wearing a hearing aid. They also noticed that Mrs. Popoff was always at the door having people fill in prayer cards and asking them things like, "Is Jesus going to heal you? What's your name? Where do you live? Have you had this condition long?" Randi brought in a radio scanner; at 39.17 MHz, he heard "the voice of God". The only problem was that God sounded like a woman. It was Popoff's wife! When Randi heard her say, "Honey, I'm looking up names now," he knew he was onto something.

ABC news went in with Randi and recorded a whole evening. They played it twice on their broadcast. The first-time viewers saw it as any member of Popoff's audience would have, but the second time they played it, they heard Mrs. Popoff's voice instructing her husband with regard to names, addresses, ailments, and the locations of people. You would think that after Popoff was exposed, people would have nothing more to do with him. However, despite a temporary decline, his ministry is still going strong. A while ago I was shocked to see him regularly featured on television. He is still promising miracles from God - just send a faith pledge (aka. - a donation).

---

[3] http://peterpopoff.org/ministry-history (accessed May 10, 2015).

This kind of story reveals that, when it comes to miracles, people can be very gullible. Moreover, in the name of religion, this gullibility can be manipulated. Thomas, however, was a skeptic who refused to be taken in, swindled, or deceived by such religious deception.

Note that the specific evidence Thomas asked for could not be faked. First, Thomas would not believe a second-hand story; he had to see Jesus for himself. Second, Thomas had to see the nail marks in Jesus' hands and touch him. This would not only ensure Jesus was not a ghost, but it would also narrow the field of potential candidates claiming to be resurrected. The Romans did not nail all of their crucifixion victims to crosses; many were simply tied with ropes. For Thomas to see fresh nail prints in the hands of the man claiming to be the resurrected Jesus would rule out just about everyone but Jesus himself. Finally, Thomas asked for something that was unique to Jesus, namely, that he put his hand into Jesus' side. To understand this we must remember that the Romans were experts at execution. To ensure their crucified victims were dead, after hours or days of torture, they would break their legs. This action would result in the victim's inability to push himself up to take a breath and he would quickly die of asphyxiation. However, this did not happen to Jesus, because he died after a few hours, thus making it unnecessary to break his legs. Just to ensure Jesus was truly dead, one of the soldiers drove a spear through his side, puncturing his lungs and heart.

> The soldiers therefore came and broke the legs of the first man who had been crucified with Jesus, and then those of the other. But when they came to Jesus and found that he was already dead, they did not break his legs. Instead, one of the soldiers

pierced Jesus' side with a spear, bringing a sudden flow of blood and water.[4]

Thomas demanded these three proofs because he wanted incontrovertible evidence that the Jesus who appeared to the disciples was the same Jesus who died on the cross and not a ghost or some look-alike who was trying to defraud everyone. Thomas was adamant that he would not believe if he did not receive this empirical evidence.

THE TRANSFORMATION OF THOMAS

Second, John asks us to consider the life transformation of "doubting Thomas". John claims that Thomas was immediately changed as a result of seeing Jesus.

> A week later his disciples were in the house again, and Thomas was with them. Though the doors were locked, Jesus came and stood among them and said, "Peace be with you!" Then he said to Thomas, "Put your finger here; see my hands. Reach out your hand and put it into my side. Stop doubting and believe."[5]

Note the exact parallels between Thomas's original demands and what Jesus commanded Thomas to do. Thomas said, "Unless I see the nail marks in his hands and put my finger where the nails were…" and Jesus said, "Put your finger here; see my hands." Thomas said, "Unless I put my hand into his side…" and Jesus said, "Reach out your hand and put it into my side." Thomas said, "I will not believe it," and Jesus said, "Stop doubting and believe."

---

[4] John 19:32-34.
[5] John 20:26-27.

Thomas's transformation was immediate. The skeptic instantly became a believer. His response summarizes the change: "Thomas said to him, 'My Lord and my God!' "[6] Do not misread Thomas's response as a shocked teenager texting, "OMG!" Ancient people did not use such phrases. Thomas claimed that the man who appeared to him *was*, indeed, Jesus and that this resurrected Jesus was God himself. It would be astounding for anyone to call another man "God", but for a Jew to worship a man as God was simply shocking. If Jesus is not God, Thomas was guilty of blasphemy. Yet Thomas worshipped Jesus as God.

At first glance this response seems a little strange. If this really is Jesus, why did Thomas not say, "You're alive!" or at least "Sorry about that, Jesus."? Why respond with "My Lord and my God"? The best clue comes earlier in the story when John tells us this event took place a week *after* Jesus first appeared to the disciples.[7] In other words, Thomas had to endure a week of hearing his best friends say, "We have seen the Lord!"[8] We have to wonder what Thomas was thinking during that time. D.A. Carson suggests that, just as any bereaved person thinks about their loved one, Thomas would have been recalling the last three years of his life with Jesus. He would have been thinking about all the things he had experienced with Jesus, while at the same time wondering if there were any possible reality to the claims of the other disciples.

Perhaps he recalled the day when Jesus said to a paralyzed man, "Son, your sins are forgiven."[9] After Jesus said this, some teachers of the law who were sitting there said, "Why does this

---

[6] John 20:28.
[7] John 20:26 – "A week later his disciples were in the house again, and Thomas was with them."
[8] John 20:25.
[9] Mark 2:5.

fellow talk like that? He's blaspheming! Who can forgive sins but God alone?"[10] They were correct to respond this way. In order to understand why, imagine you were mugged so badly that you were hospitalized. Now imagine that I then went and found the perpetrators and said to them, "Your sins are forgiven." You would say to me, "How dare you? You cannot forgive them. I am the one who was mugged. I am the only one who can offer them forgiveness." In the same way, the Scriptures that the teachers of the law studied taught that all sin is ultimately against God and therefore only God can ultimately forgive sins. Yet here was Jesus telling a man that his sins were forgiven.[11]

Perhaps Thomas also recalled the time Jesus spoke and the weather obeyed him, the time he walked into a funeral and caused a dead man to sit up in his coffin, the time water suddenly turned into the finest of wines, or the time the five loaves and two fish multiplied to feed five thousand people.

As Thomas removed his hand from the scar in this man's side, he suddenly believed that this was no mere man standing in front of him. Nor did he believe this was the greatest of all men. He believed that this man was otherworldly and beyond the natural realm. This man was supernatural. In that moment, Thomas believed he was in the presence of deity and burst into worship saying, "My Lord and my God!"

Whether you believe Thomas's story or not, you must at least give consideration to our collective bias against ancient people. This chapter and the previous one have endeavoured to show that, far from being inclined to believe in the resurrection of Jesus, these ancient and "pre-scientific" people seem to be just as disinclined to believe as we are today.

---

[10] Mark 2:7.
[11] This illustration borrowed from Carson, *Scandalous*, 143-168.

Chapter 9
Our Bias Against God Himself

I want atheism to be true…It isn't just that I don't believe in God…I don't want there to be a God; I don't want the universe to be like that.[1]

- philosopher and atheist Thomas Nagel

If "doubting Thomas" is right – that Jesus really is the resurrected Son of God then the entire discussion of miracles suddenly takes a terrifying twist. If miracles are true it means we are not alone in the universe. There is Someone else "in the box" with us. It is quite shocking to suddenly realize, as Thomas did, that God himself is among us.

C.S. Lewis compares this to the shock you feel in smaller matters: the shock that occurs when suddenly the fishing rod pulls back at you; when something breathes beside you in the

---

[1] Thomas Nagel, *The Last Word* (Oxford: Oxford University Press, 1996), 130.

dark; when a twig breaks when you thought you were all alone in the forest; when you were just playing cops and robbers but suddenly your sister says, "Ssh! Be quiet! I think I just heard *real* footsteps in the hallway." It is always shocking to realize you are not alone when you were certain that you *were* alone - to realize that something or someone has invaded your space. If we were to encounter a true miracle, we would suddenly realize that God himself exists – that he is pulling at the other end of the line, that he is the one hunting us in the forest, that he is in our hallway, and that he has been there all along.[2]

This is terrifying to us because it would mean we are not alone. Moreover, if we are not alone - if God himself has invaded our space - then we must reevaluate everything in light of who this God is and anything this God might require of us. This is unnerving to us. What if this God seeks to guide us on how to live, how to think, how to act, how to spend our money, how to relate to him, and how we should and should not use our sexuality?

A BIAS UNDER OUR BIASES?

Could it be that our bias against miracles is actually a bias against God himself? When people are really honest, they admit this bias against God. Philosopher Thomas Nagel of NYU candidly writes, "I want atheism to be true...It isn't just that I don't believe in God...I don't want there to be a God; I don't want the universe to be like that."[3] C.S. Lewis admitted the same bias before he became a Christian: "I had always wanted, above all things, not to be 'interfered with.' "[4]

---

[2] This paragraph paraphrases and adds to C.S. Lewis, *Miracles* (New York: Touchstone, 1996), 124-125.

[3] Nagel, *The Last Word*, 130.

[4] C.S. Lewis, *Surprised by Joy* (Orlando: Harcourt Inc., 1955), 228.

Aldous Huxley, a humanist of the 20ᵗʰ century, was honest about the fact his contemporaries rejected God because they wanted to be free to live life as they desired and that, for a time, he followed this philosophy as well.

> I had motives for not wanting the world to have a meaning; consequently assumed that it had none, and was able without any difficulty to find satisfying reasons for this assumption…The philosopher who finds no meaning in the world is not concerned exclusively with a problem in pure metaphysics, he is also concerned to prove that there is no valid reason why he personally should not do as he wants to do…For myself, as, no doubt, for most of my contemporaries, the philosophy of meaninglessness was essentially an instrument of liberation. The liberation we desired was simultaneously liberation from a certain political and economic system and liberation from a certain system of morality. We objected to the morality because it interfered with our sexual freedom; we objected to the political and economic system because it was unjust. The supporters of these systems claimed that in some way they embodied the meaning (a Christian meaning, they insisted) of the world. There was one admirably simple method of confuting these people and at the same time justifying ourselves in our political and erotical revolt: we could deny that the world had any meaning whatsoever.[5]

---

[5] Aldous Huxley, *Ends and Means: An Enquiry into the Nature of Ideals and into the Methods Employed for Their Realization* (London, Chatto and Windus, 1941), 270, 272-73. A pdf of the book can be accessed at: http://cdn.preterhuman.net/texts/religion.occult.new_age/occult.conspirac y.and.related/Huxley,%20Aldous%20-%20Ends%20And%20Means.pdf (accessed May 10, 2015).

A GOD WHO SEEKS OUR GOOD

Christianity speaks directly to this bias against God by asserting that the God who invades our space is seeking our good. John states that he records Thomas' story for a reason: "Jesus did many other miraculous signs in the presence of his disciples, which are not recorded in this book. But these are written that you may believe that Jesus is the Christ, the Son of God, and that by believing *you may have life in his name*."[6] Christianity says that the reason God invaded our space (as if it were ever "ours" to begin with), and walked among us as the historical person named Jesus, was to bring us "life." In the words of Jesus himself, "I have come that they may have life, and have it to the full."[7] Jesus demonstrated this by the way he cared for others, showed compassion, included the outsider, healed bodies, taught truth, and rebuked hypocrisy. Furthermore, Christianity teaches that in his death and miraculous resurrection, Jesus defeated sin, evil, and death in order that we might be reunited with God both now and for eternity. In other words, Christianity teaches that all true miracles are God acting in this world to bring about good things for humanity.

SUMMARY

In the chapters on *Miracles & Science* I have asked you to consider the idea that our refusal to believe in miracles is not the result of following scientific evidence to its logical conclusion; rather it is the consequence of presupposed biases that have little, if anything, to do with science.

We began by looking at our bias against supernaturalism. Here we saw that the debate about miracles is actually a debate about

---

[6] John 20:30-31.
[7] John 10:10.

the existence of God; if God exists then it is perfectly reasonable to believe that he can act in miraculous ways within the universe he created and sustains. Therefore, unless we can unquestionably prove that God does not exist, we must, at the very least, be open to the possibility of miracles.

Second, we considered our bias toward scientism. We made the critical distinction between science (which explains how the universe works) and scientism (which just like other "isms" believes science can ultimately explain everything) in order to show that science is limited in what it can explain. This is confirmed by the fact that science cannot answer some of our most basic and important questions; questions like why we are here, what makes an action right or wrong, and what makes something beautiful. Furthermore, since science cannot ultimately prove or disprove the existence or non-existence of God, it cannot ultimately decide if God works miracles in the universe.

Third, we considered our bias against ancient people. Modern people often disregard ancient people's testimony about miracles, because we assume pre-scientific people were more inclined to believe miraculous stories than we are today. We saw, however, that, as is true today, some ancient people were gullible and superstitious; we saw that, as is true today, the ancient world was also filled with skeptical people. When it came to the resurrection of Jesus, we discovered that ancient people were just as skeptical, if not more so, than we are today. Despite this cynicism, many, like Thomas, came to believe. We cannot, therefore, immediately discount the testimony of ancient people as pre-scientific gullibility; rather, we must give their claims a fair hearing.

Finally, we asked if our resistance to miracles does not, in fact, reveal a deeper bias against God himself. If miracles do occur, it follows that we are not alone in the universe. This means that we must reevaluate everything in light of who God is and what he might require of us. Although this is unnerving to us, Christianity's central miraculous claim is that God became a man – not to harm us – but to bring us life now and forevermore.

It is my hope that as you investigate Christianity, and particularly its miraculous claims about Jesus Christ, you will give critical reflection to the collective biases we have against the existence of miracles.

PROBLEM #3:
VIOLENCE & GOD

WHY SHOULD I WORSHIP A GOD WHO COMMANDED GENOCIDE?

INTRODUCTION

The attacks of September 11, 2001 raised our level of consciousness regarding violence committed in the name of religion. In a post 9-11 world, the connection between religion and violence has led to questions about Christianity that were not as common twenty years ago. Generally speaking, when people used to disagree with Christianity, they still spoke with an overall respect for the God of the Bible. However, many are now loudly declaring the God of the Bible to be a moral monster who should not be afforded any respect at all.[1]

The problem with Christianity, according to these voices, is the immoral character of God in commanding the use of violence. One of the primary examples used to prove this point is God's command for Israel to destroy the nations living in Canaan. Deuteronomy 20:16-20 provides a succinct summary of God's directives:

> …in the cities of the nations the Lord your God is giving you as an inheritance, do not leave alive anything that breathes. Completely destroy them—the Hittites, Amorites, Canaanites, Perizzites, Hivites and Jebusites—as the Lord your God has commanded you. Otherwise, they will teach you to follow all the detestable things they do in worshiping their gods, and you will sin against the Lord your God.

---

[1] This change of attitude is generally due to "the new atheists" who, as a direct response to 9-11, released books in which they sought to show that religion leads to violence. See Richard Dawkins' *The God Delusion*, Sam Harris' *The End Of* Faith, Daniel Dennett's *Breaking the Spell*, and Christopher Hitchen's *god Is Not Great*.

Alistair McGrath writes: "The take-home message of Dawkins's recent book, *The God Delusion* can be summarized very simply: religion causes bombings! Get rid of religion, and the greatest threat to global peace and security will be eliminated." Ravi Zacharias ed., *Beyond Opinion: Living the Faith that We Defend* (Nashville: Thomas Nelson, 2007), 27.

The book of Joshua goes on to describe how Israel, at the command of God, invaded and conquered the Canaanites. This, people say, is genocide. It proves God is an unjust moral monster who should be utterly rejected. Richard Dawkins refers to the war on Canaan as "ethnic cleansing"[2]. He says:

> ...the Bible story of Joshua's destruction of Jericho, and the invasion of the Promised Land in general, is morally indistinguishable from Hitler's invasion of Poland, or Saddam Hussein's massacres of the Kurds and the Marsh Arabs...Do not think, by the way, the God character in the story nurses any doubts or scruples about the massacres and genocides that accompanied the seizing of the Promised Land.[3]

In light of this, Dawkins accuses God of being an "evil monster"[4] and minces no words in expressing his assessment of God's character:

> The God of the Old Testament is arguably the most unpleasant character in all fiction: jealous and proud of it; a petty, unjust, unforgiving control-freak; a vindictive, *bloodthirsty ethnic cleanser*, a misogynistic, homophobic, racist, infanticidal, *genocidal*, filicidal, pestilential, megalomaniacal, sadomasochistic, capriciously malevolent bully.[5]

In like manner, Christopher Hitchens recalls that the Canaanites were "pitilessly driven out of their homes to make room for the ungrateful and mutinous children of Israel", and

---

[2] Richard Dawkins, *The God Delusion* (Boston: Houghton Mifflin Company, 2008), 280.

[3] Dawkins, *The God Delusion*, 280.

[4] Dawkins, *The God Delusion*, 282.

[5] Dawkins, *The God Delusion*, 51. Emphasis mine.

asserts that the Bible "contain[s] a warrant for ethnic cleansing...and for indiscriminate massacre."[6]

Since God's command of violence against the Canaanites is one of the primary examples cited in accusing God of being unjust, this book will examine the question, "Is God an evil monster for commanding violence against the Canaanites?" In chapter 10 we will take a closer look at the Bible's own oft-neglected backstory for God's violence against the Canaanites. In chapter 11 we will unpack the Bible's justification for the violence of God against the Canaanites. This chapter will demonstrate that God's destruction of the Canaanites was not an arbitrary and capricious outbreak of anger but was a response to centuries of Canaanite wrongdoing. Finally, in chapter 12, we will consider how Jesus' violent death provides a shocking twist in the Bible's story that reveals the true character of God.

---

[6] Hitchens, *god Is Not Great*, 101-102.

Chapter 10
The Bible's Backstory
For The Violence Of God

Have you ever started watching a movie when it is almost over? It is a very frustrating experience. Why did the angry man shoot the other guy who seemed to be so nice? If you are watching the movie on television you likely changed the channel. If you walk into the room while others are watching, you will probably just go to another room until it is over. The problem, of course, is that you don't know the whole story. If you had seen the movie from the beginning, it would have made perfect sense. The angry man was an undercover police officer and the "nice" man had abducted a child.

Knowing the whole story changes everything and so it is with the question of the violence of God. The Bible gives its own backstory for why God ordered the destruction of the Canaanites but it is given much earlier in the Bible's story. Those who accuse God of being an evil monster quite possibly have not considered this backstory and therefore have not placed the violence of God within its proper context. If we are going to understand the command of God to destroy the Canaanites, we must recall the Bible's context – the Bible's backstory to this event.

THE BIBLE'S BACKSTORY

The Bible's story begins in Genesis, chapters 1-3, with the declaration that God created everything that exists but that human beings rebelled against their Creator. Chapters 4-11 chronicle the terrible effects of what life is like when humanity turns its collective back on God. They are filled with things like murder, arrogance, revenge, violence, and incest. But the story takes a radical shift in Genesis 12. God reveals himself to a man named Abram (later to be called "Abraham"). God promises Abram that his descendants will become a great nation, through whom God further promises to bless "all the peoples on earth."[1] This grand plan of blessing is elaborated in Genesis 15 when God promises to give Abram's descendants the very land on which he is standing – the land of Canaan: "I am the LORD, who brought you out of Ur of the Chaldeans to give you this land to take possession of it."[2]

God tells Abraham how this will take place and, (more importantly for my purposes in this chapter), *when* it will take place: "Then the LORD said to him, 'Know for certain that your descendants will be strangers in a country not their own, and they will be enslaved and mistreated *four hundred years*. But I will punish the nation they serve as slaves, and afterward they will come out with great possessions.' "[3]

Note three things about the story so far: 1) God promises to make Abraham's descendants into a great nation (later be called "Israel") 2) God will give the land of Canaan to Israel 3) this will not happen until the Israelites have spent four hundred years as slaves in Egypt. From the moment God made this promise to Abram, it would still be approximately three

---

[1] Genesis 12:3
[2] Genesis 15:7.
[3] Genesis 15:13-14.

hundred years *until* Abraham's descendants became a nation. Abraham's wife, Sarah, still had to give birth to his son Isaac, who in turn grew up and fathered Jacob. Jacob eventually had twelve sons who then moved to Egypt. They multiplied in number, and became the nation of Israel. As noted, all of this took approximately three hundred years. It was not until *after* this three hundred year time span time that Israel was enslaved for four hundred years in Egypt. This means God did not actually give Israel the land of Canaan for about *seven hundred years* after he promised it to Abram (300 years to become the nation of Israel plus 400 years in slavery once they were a nation). The critical question is this: why wouldn't God give Israel the land of Canaan for seven hundred years? Why wait such an incredibly long time?

The Bible gives its own answer in Genesis chapter 15. Speaking again to Abram about the Amorites (the major people group in the land of Canaan during Abram's day) God says, "In the fourth generation your descendants will come back here *for the sin of the Amorites has not yet reached its full measure.*"[4] With this pronouncement we discover that the conquest of Canaan is to be understood within the justice and patience of God. First, God is extremely patient in that he does not bring the sword of justice down on the Amorites for just one sin, or even for one hundred years of sin. God waits and waits for the nations in Canaan to turn away from their sin. Second, God is just. In our society, we work patiently with criminals to rehabilitate them; if they continually break the laws, however, we eventually bring strict justice upon them. In like manner, the Bible shows that God is extremely patient in that he waits over seven hundred years for the Canaanites to turn away from their sins. Eventually, those sins cross a moral threshold and, like any just judge, God punishes them.

---

[4] Genesis 15:16b.

IS THIS GENOCIDE?

The Bible never asserts, or even hints, that the Canaanites were destroyed because of their ethnicity. It is, therefore, extremely inaccurate to say this is an act of genocide. Genocide is fueled by racial hatred. The conquest of Canaan had nothing to do with race. God did not order the destruction of the Canaanites because of their ethnicity; he destroyed them because of their sin. This is not, therefore, a case of ethnic cleansing; it is a case of capital punishment. (Depending on where one sits on the topic of capital punishment, this may be only one step on what is a very challenging moral ladder). But we must read on.

The Bible's answer for the violence of God against the Canaanites can be summarized as follows: *The conquest of Canaan was not racially motivated genocide but a command of God against a specific people living in a specific time whose wickedness had reached a tipping point.* Deuteronomy 9:5 echoes this assertion when God says to Israel, "It is not because of your righteousness or your integrity that you are going in to take possession of their land; *but on account of the wickedness of these nations,* the LORD your God will drive them out before you, to accomplish what he swore to your fathers, to Abraham, Isaac and Jacob."

JUST AND UNJUST USES OF VIOLENCE

The Bible's answer does not make the destruction of the Canaanites any less violent but it does frame the violence in a different category. There is a major difference between violence that is random or racially motivated and violence that is a just punishment for wrongdoing.[5]

---

[5] Christopher Wright, *The God I Don't Understand* (Grand Rapids: Zondervan, 2008), Kindle Edition, Location 1626.

A recent incident in Canada serves as a good illustration. On October 22, 2014 Michael Zehaf-Bibeau walked onto Parliament Hill, the centre of Canada's government. He fatally shot Cpl. Nathan Cirillo who was standing guard at the Canadian National War Memorial. He then entered the Parliament building where members of the Parliament of Canada, including the Prime Minister, were meeting. A shootout began and the Commons Sergeant at Arms, Kevin Vickers, subsequently shot and killed Zehaf-Bibeau.

In this example we see two types of violence, one of which we do not accept as morally just and the other we do accept as just, even if we believe it is always undesirable to take someone's life. We do not accept Zehaf-Bibeau's using violence to shoot Cpl. Cirillo in cold blood. However, most people accept Kevin Vickers's using violence to kill Zehaf-Bibeau. This does not mean that we think the violence Kevin Vickers used is nice or pleasant but it does mean that most accept it as a necessary and just act.

Likewise, each Remembrance Day (for Canadians) or Veterans' Day (for Americans) we are reminded of the violence of World War II. As we recall these events, we *do not* accept the violence of the Nazis in systematically murdering six million Jews. Yet again, most people *do* accept the violence of the Allied nations in defeating Hitler's forces. Old Testament scholar Christopher Wright says, "The fact that the Bible insists repeatedly that the violence of the conquest was inflicted as an act of punishment on a whole society puts it in a moral framework that must be differentiated from random or ethnocentric genocide. It does not make it "nice", but it does make it different."[6]

---

[6] Wright, *The God I Don't Understand*, Location 1632.

WHAT ACTUALLY HAPPENED IN CANAAN?

After fourty years of wandering in the wilderness, Israel's military was vast in number, armed to the teeth, and ready to fight. The Canaanites, lulled into a false sense of security by their idyllic paradise "flowing with milk and honey"[7], were caught by surprise. In a blitzkrieg of shock and awe, the Israelites used their superior power to crush the peaceful but naïve Canaanites. Israel's onslaught must have been a spectacular display of force as city after city was overpowered and the Canaanite population exterminated.

This is the story most people imagine in their minds. The only problem is that such a story is precisely that – imagination. History paints a very different picture. There are four factors that, properly understood, should cause us to think very differently about what actually happened in Canaan.[8]

First, Israel was a nation of slaves who dared to go up against a violently oppressive empire, not an army routing a peace-loving Canaanite people. Israel had just come out of four hundred years of slavery and had been wandering in the wilderness for forty years. This ragtag group of ex-slaves was up against a world super power that had engulfed and destroyed other nations. Israel was outgunned and outmanned for Canaan had heavily fortified military outposts (such as Jericho), as well as the most advanced weaponry of their day. Joshua Butler writes,

---

[7] Exodus 33:3.

[8] For a more detailed discussion of the subsequent paragraphs see: Paul Copan, *Is God a Moral Monster? Making Sense of the Old Testament God* (Grand Rapids: Baker Books, 2011), chapters 15-17; Christopher Wright, *The God I Don't Understand* (Grand Rapids: Zondervan, 2008), chapters 4-5; Joshua Butler, *The Skeletons in God's Closet: The Mercy of Hell, the Surprise of Judgment, the Hope of Holy War* (Nashville: Thomas Nelson, 2014), chapters 13-18.

You expect the grade-school bully to take on the weakling with lunch money; you don't expect him to take on the high school wrestling team. You expect a pirate to capture a vessel lost at sea; you don't expect him to declare war on the Spanish Aramada. You expect a Third World dictator to abuse scattered dissenters; you don't expect him to hop in his personal jet and take on the US Air Force...Israel is a nation of fearful, intimidated slaves facing off with the mightiest imperial powerhouses of the ancient world.[9]

This is why Israel sang, "Some trust in chariots and some in horses, but we trust in the name of the Lord our God."[10] Israel's only hope was that God would come through on his promise to deliver the land of Canaan to them.

Second, Israel attacked military strongholds, not concentrated civilian populations. In the ancient Middle East, most people lived in the countryside. The "cities" of Canaan (such as Jericho and Ai), were not like modern cities where people gather to live and do business. Rather, cities were military outposts used to guard the civilian populations living beyond them, much like the Great Wall of China was built to protect the people on the inside of the wall. Jericho, for example, was positioned at the junction of three roads leading to the cities of Jerusalem, Bethel and Orpah, and thus protected the Jordan Valley and the hill country beyond. Israel's violence, therefore, was directed toward the military installments; against the combatants and their kings stationed there.[11] Dr. Paul Copan writes,

---

[9] Joshua Butler, *The Skeletons in God's Closet: The Mercy of Hell, the Surprise of Judgment, the Hope of Holy War* (Nashville: Thomas Nelson, 2014), Kindle Edition, Location 3733.

[10] Psalm 20:7.

[11] The continual references to kings also demonstrate this. In Old Testament times, a king was not a king in the sense we know kings today. He was a military leader subordinate to a higher official who lived elsewhere.

All the archeological evidence indicates that no civilian populations existed at Jericho, Ai, and other cities mentioned in Joshua...Jericho was a small settlement of probably one hundred or fewer soldiers. This is why all of Israel could circle it seven times and then do battle against it on the same day.[12]

Joshua Butler summarizes: "So when Israel 'utterly destroys' a city like Jericho or Ai, we should picture a military fort being taken over – not a civilian massacre. God is pulling down the Great Wall of China, not demolishing Beijing."[13]

Third, the language of total destruction was an ancient form of warfare rhetoric that is somewhat akin to "trash talk" in our contemporary sporting world. The Bible speaks of Israel's victory in all-encompassing terms: "Thus Joshua struck all the land...he left no survivor, but he utterly destroyed all who breathed."[14] Yet, as will be demonstrated, Joshua himself acknowledges that this is not literally the case. Is he lying? No, he is simply using the accepted warfare rhetoric of his day.

This rhetoric is similar to the language the sporting world uses in our present day. If our hockey team beats the rival team 7-2, we say, "We killed them! They couldn't do anything against us! We totally destroyed them!" If such talk is taken literally, it sounds as if the other team hardly got a shot on goal, let alone put two pucks behind our goaltender. Taken literally, such grandiose language makes it sound like our team won 19-0, but we all understand the context of this kind of rhetoric. No one is lying or seeking to deceive; it is simply an accepted, figurative way of speaking – hyperbole.

---

[12] Paul Copan, *Is God a Moral Monster? Making Sense of the Old Testament God* (Grand Rapids: Baker Books, 2011), 176.
[13] Butler, *Skeletons in God's Closet*, Location 3947.
[14] Joshua 10:40.

In like manner, the language in the book of Joshua conformed to the accepted warfare rhetoric of his day. For instance, the Egyptian Tuthmosis III (later fifteenth century BC) bragged, "…the numerous army of Mitanni was overthrown within the hour, annihilated totally, like those (now) not existent." In reality, Mitanni's armies were not totally destroyed; they fought throughout the fifteenth and fourteenth centuries BC.[15]

The same type of language (hyperbole) appears in Joshua. For example, Joshua 11:21 states, "At that time Joshua went and destroyed the Anakites from the hill country: from Hebron, Debir and Anab, from all the hill country of Judah, and from all the hill country of Israel. Joshua totally destroyed them and their towns. No Anakites were left in Israelite territory." Yet only three chapters later, this very same Joshua gives Caleb permission to drive out the Anakites in the "hill country" who possess "cities" that are "large and fortified."[16]

Although the book of Joshua speaks in terms of total destruction, the end of the book assumes the continued existence of the Canaanites, because Joshua warns the Israelites about following their destructive ways.[17] Likewise, Deuteronomy 7:2 commands Israel to "defeat" and "utterly destroy" the Canaanites and yet goes on in verses 3-5 to command them not to intermarry or make treaties with the Canaanites they "destroy." Copan summarizes the point:

> A closer look at the biblical text reveals a lot more nuance – and a lot less bloodshed. In short, the conquest of Canaan was far less widespread and harsh than many people assume. Like his ancient Near Eastern contemporaries, Joshua used the language of conventional warfare rhetoric…he was speaking the language

---

[15] Copan, *Is God a Moral Monster?*, 172.
[16] Joshua 14:12-14.
[17] See Josh 23:7, 12-13; cf 15:63; 16:10; 17:13; Judges 2:10-13.

that everyone in his day would have understood...The language is typically exaggerated and full of bravado, depicting total devastation. The knowing ancient Near Eastern reader recognized this as hyperbole; the accounts weren't understood to be literally true...Joshua was just saying he had fairly well trounced the enemy.[18]

Finally, Israel's conquest of Canaan is described more in terms of "driving out" than of "killing off." To drive out means to expel or eject, which assumes the people were alive – not dead. God, like a landlord whose patience with his unruly tenants has run out, was kicking out the Canaanites. The references to driving out/dispossessing are, in fact, more numerous than the references to destroying.[19]

- "The LORD will drive out all these nations before you, and you will dispossess nations larger and stronger than you."[20]

- "Little by little I will drive them out before you, until you have increased enough to take possession of the land."[21]

- "The LORD has driven out before you great and powerful nations; to this day no one has been able to withstand you."[22]

---

[18] Copan, *Is God a Moral Monster?*, 170-171.
[19] "Driving out or dispossessing is different from wiping out or destroying. Explusion is in view, not annihilation (eg. 'dispossess [*yarash*]' in Exod. 34:24; Num 32:21; Deut 4:38 NET). Just as Adam and Eve were 'driven out [*garash*]' of the garden (Gen 3:24) or Cain into the wilderness (4:14) or David from Israel by Saul (1 Sam 26:19), so the Israelites were to 'dispossess' the Canaanites." Copan, *Is God a Moral Monster?*, 181.
[20] Deuteronomy 11:23.
[21] Exodus 23:30.
[22] Joshua 23:9.

SUMMARY

This chapter has shown that much of our reaction to God's command for the Israelites to use violence against the Canaanites is misguided. God's command had nothing to do with racially motivated genocide. Neither should we imagine the Canaanites as a peaceful people who were annihilated by a bloodthirsty Israelite empire following the commands of a vindictive God. The Bible's answer for the violence of God is to be found in the fact that this was the just punishment of God against a culture whose wickedness had reached a tipping point.

But what did the Canaanites do that deserved this? Were they really that bad? This is the subject of the next chapter.

Chapter 11
The Bible's Justification
For The Violence Of God

In this chapter I want to give you a sampling of the evidence
that led God to order the destruction of the Canaanites. Just as
juries are often required to see and hear things that are
disturbing, you, as jury members in the case of the Canaanites,
are about to read some things that are quite graphic. Although
this may be disturbing, it is necessary, for we cannot
understand the justness of God in punishing the Canaanites
unless we first feel the force of their crimes.

The Bible passages we have already quoted broadly summarize
the evidence:

> It is not because of your righteousness or your integrity that you
> are going in to take possession of their land; *but on account of the*
> *wickedness of these nations*, the LORD your God will drive them out
> before you, to accomplish what he swore to your fathers, to
> Abraham, Isaac and Jacob.[1]

---

[1] Deuteronomy 9:5.

…in the cities of the nations the LORD your God is giving you as an inheritance, do not leave alive anything that breathes. Completely destroy them—the Hittites, Amorites, Canaanites, Perizzites, Hivites and Jebusites—as the LORD your God has commanded you. Otherwise, they will teach you to follow *all the detestable things they do in worshiping their gods*, and you will sin against the LORD your God.[2]

The Bible argues that the "detestable things" the Canaanites did were a direct result of "worshipping their gods." The Canaanites were proof of the old maxim that we become what we behold; "what people revere, they resemble, either for ruin or restoration."[3] The Bible and archeological evidence document the "detestable things" the Canaanites did as they became like the gods they worshipped.[4]

CANAANITE INCEST

Since the gods of Canaanite worship were incestuous, the people also practised incest. The god El, who was the father of the Canaanite gods, had seventy children by Asherah. Two of those children were Baal and Anat. In one story, Baal tells his father, El, that his mother, Asherah, had tried to seduce him. El tells Baal to have sex with her in order to humiliate her, which Baal does. Baal also has sex with his own daughter. This

---

[2] Deuteronomy 20:16-18.

[3] Gregory Beale, *We Become What We Worship* (Downers Grove: IVP Press, 2008),16.

[4] Large sections of this chapter borrow heavily from Clay Jones, "We don't hate sin so we don't understand what happened to the Canaanites," *Philosophia Christi* 11, no. 1 (2009): 53-72.

practice was not condemned in Canaanite culture; in fact, it was considered acceptable.[5]

Canaanite incest is reported in the biblical story of Sodom. After this Canaanite city was destroyed, Lot's daughters (Canaanite women) got him drunk and had sex with him in order to propagate the family line:

> That night they got their father to drink wine, and the older daughter went in and lay with him. He was not aware of it when she lay down or when she got up. The next day the older daughter said to the younger, "Last night I lay with my father. Let's get him to drink wine again tonight, and you go in and lie with him so we can preserve our family line through our father." So they got their father to drink wine that night also, and the younger daughter went and lay with him. Again he was not aware of it when she lay down or when she got up. So both of Lot's daughters became pregnant by their father.[6]

CANAANITE TEMPLE SEX

Baal was represented by the phallic symbol of an upright stone. Carved female figurines with exaggerated breasts and prominent genitals represented the goddess Astarte. In Canaanite thinking, the productivity of the land depended upon the sexual relationship between Baal and his female companion. It was believed that, when Baal and Astarte had intercourse, the

---

[5] We also see this approval of incest within other local cultures of the time. There is an Egyptian book, written for men, that tells them how to interpret the everyday relevance of their dreams: "If a man sees himself in a dream…having intercourse with his mother. Good. His companions will stick to him…having intercourse with his sister: Good. It means he will inherit something. Having intercourse with a woman: Bad. It means mourning." Jones, *Philosophia Christi*, 58.

[6] Genesis 19:33-36.

rains (Baal's semen) would fall to the earth and cause the crops to flourish.

To encourage the gods, a Canaanite man would go to a Baal shrine and have intercourse with one of the sacred prostitutes. The man would play Baal's role while the prostitute played Astarte's role. Often the worshippers would engage in a massive orgy trying to coax the gods into having sex.

One story tells of El, the father of the gods, having sex with two goddesses. The story ends with the following directions for those gathered at the temple: "To be repeated five times by the company and the singers of the assembly."[7] As a matter of civic duty, men – married or single – were expected to engage in temple sex. To do otherwise would cause a man to be seen as hindering the local economy.

CANAANITE CHILD SACRIFICE

God commanded his people not to copy the child sacrifice practices of the Canaanites: "Do not give any of your children to be sacrificed to Molech."[8] Molech was a Canaanite god of the underworld who was represented as a man with a bull's head. Statues of Molech portrayed him in a standing position with his arms outstretched over a cauldron of fire. Children were placed in his arms where they would burn to death. These were not just unwanted babies, but infants and children up to the age of four.

> Kleitarchos says the Phoenicians and especially the
> Carthaginians who honored Kronos [another name for Molech],
> whenever they wished to succeed in any great enterprise, would

---

[7] Jones, *Philosophia Christi*, 60.
[8] Leviticus 18:22.

---

vow by one of their children if they achieved the things they longed for, to sacrifice him to a god. A bronze image of Kronos was set up among them, stretching out its cupped hands above a bronze cauldron, which would burn the child. As the flame burning the child surrounded the body, the limbs would shrivel up and the mouth would appear to grin as if laughing, until it was shrunk enough to slip into the cauldron.[9]

The ancient historian, Plutarch, reports that during Canaanite sacrifices, "the whole area before the statue was filled with a loud noise of flutes and drums so that the cries of the wailing should not reach the ears of the people."[10]

CANAANITE VIOLENCE

The gods and goddesses of Canaanite culture were obsessed with violence and war. In William Albright's book, *Archeology and the Religion of Israel,* he writes about clay plaques that describe the goddess Anath. Anath, the patroness of both sex and war, drank the blood of her victims and sat surrounded by corpses. Albright describes a story of Anath massacring people in the following gory scene:

> Besides being patronesses of sexual life these interesting ladies were also goddesses of war. Anath is depicted...as a naked woman astride a galloping horse, brandishing a shield and lance in her out flung hands. In the Baal epic there is a harrowing description of Anath's thirst for blood. For a reason that still escapes us she decided to carry out a general massacre: "with might she hewed down the people of the cities, she smote the folk of the sea-coast, she slew the men of the sunrise." After filling her temple with men, she barred the gates so that none

---

[9] Jones, *Philosophia Christi,* 61.
[10] Jones, *Philosophia Christi,* 61.

might escape after which "she hurled chairs at the youth, tables at the warriors, footstools at the men of might". The blood was so deep that she waded in it up to her knees-nay, up to her neck. Under her feet were human heads, above her human hands flew like locusts. In her sensuous delight she decorated herself with suspended heads, while she attached hands to her girdle. Her joy at the butchery is described in even more sadistic language: "Her liver swelled with laughter. Her heart was full of joy. The liver of Anath was full of exultation." Afterwards, Anath "was satisfied" and washed her hands in human gore before proceeding to other occupations.[11]

CANAANITE BESTIALITY

Finally, the Canaanites practised bestiality. Again, those who practised this did so because their gods engaged in it. In a poem about Baal we read the following:

> Mightiest Baal hears;
> He makes love with a heifer in the outback,
> A cow in the field of Death's realm,
> He lies with her seventy times seven,
> Mounts eighty times eight;
> she conceives and bears a boy.[12]

There were no prohibitions against bestiality within Canaanite culture. In fact, if a man was unable to achieve or sustain an erection, it was believed he was bewitched. He would then have to perform certain rituals to remove the curse. Some of these rituals involved convincing a woman to have sex with an animal. One such ritual proscribes that an animal be tied to a

---

[11] William F. Albright, *Archeology and the Religion of Israel* (Baltimore: John Hopkins Press, 1968), 76-77.
[12] Jones, *Philosophia Christi*, 64.

bed; a woman then would speak to the animal saying, "At my head a buck is tied. At my feet [a ram is tied! Buck caress me! [Ram, copulate with me!]"[13] Dr. Jones writes, "How this continues is so disgusting that I cannot relate it."[14]

So, ladies and gentlemen of the jury, after considering this sampling of evidence, what is your view of the Canaanites? Did God have any grounds for punishing them? The Bible argues that Canaanite culture degenerated in this way for seven hundred years! During this time, God patiently waited for the people to turn away from such practices; eventually, however, justice demanded that he act. We can see then that the Bible is never asking us to view the destruction of the Canaanites as a *nice* thing; punishment is never *nice*. The Bible is, however, asking us to view God's actions as just acts against a morally degenerate culture.

WHAT KIND OF GOD DO YOU ACTUALLY WANT?

Despite all that has been said, we may still react negatively against what God did to the Canaanites. But what would you have wanted God to do? When evil happens in the world, people often shake their fist at God and say, "How can I believe in you when you allow evil in the world? Why don't you stop those who rape women, enslave children, behead journalists, or shoot Canadian soldiers on Parliament Hill?" In other words, people say, "I can't believe in a God who *doesn't* put a stop to evil." However, when it comes to a case such as the Canaanites, in which God did stop their evil practices, we suddenly take the opposite position and say, "I can't believe in a God who *does* put a stop to evil. What God did to the Canaanites was not fair. Why was God so harsh in punishing

---

[13] Jones, *Philosophia Christi*, 65.
[14] Jones, *Philosophia Christi*, 65.

them?" So do you want God to stop evil or don't you? You can't have it both ways. You can't say, "God, I won't worship you because you *don't* punish evil" and then say, "God I won't worship you because you *do* punish evil."[15]

Still, many will say, "I cannot accept all this talk of God's wrath and punishment. I believe in a God of love and tolerance, not a God of anger and judgement." But is a non-wrathful, non-judgmental God truly a loving God? Miroslav Volf, the Yale theologian who lived through the nightmare of ethnic strife in Yugoslavia, writes the following:

> I used to think that wrath was unworthy of God. Isn't God love? Shouldn't divine love be beyond wrath? God is love, and God loves every person and every creature. That's exactly why God is wrathful against some of them. My last resistance to the idea of God's wrath was a casualty of the war in the former Yugoslavia, the region from which I come. According to some estimates, 200,000 people were killed and over 3,000,000 were displaced. *My* villages and cities were destroyed, *my* people shelled day in and day out, some of them brutalized beyond imagination, and I could not imagine God not being angry…How did God react to the carnage? By doting on the perpetrators in a grandfatherly fashion? By refusing to condemn the bloodbath but instead affirming the perpetrators basic goodness? Wasn't God fiercely angry with them? Though I used to complain about the indecency of the idea of God's wrath, I came to think that I would have to rebel against a God who *wasn't* wrathful at the sight of the world's evil. God isn't wrathful in spite of being love. God is wrathful *because* God is love.[16]

---

[15] I once heard Dr. Timothy Keller make a similar argument and although I cannot locate when or where he said it, I give him credit for getting me to think along these lines.

[16] Miroslav Volf, *Free of Charge: Giving and Forgiving in a Culture Stripped of Grace* (Grand Rapids: Zondervan, 2006), 138-139.

SUMMARY

The goal of this chapter has been to show that, although God is extremely patient, he is also just. God cares about good and evil and will therefore not allow sin to go unpunished. He will, eventually, act to punish those who continue in gratuitous sin. For example, he will not allow the slaughter of babies to go on indefinitely; he will eventually bring justice on those who commit such atrocities.

This section on *Violence and God* could conclude with this chapter. But, the Bible's larger story will not allow us to leave this discussion at a strictly theoretical level. The Bible asserts that the story of God's patience and justice with the Canaanites has everything to do with us who live in the 21st century. This is the subject of the next chapter.

Chapter 12
The Bible's Shocking Twist
Concerning The Violence Of God

What would *The Lord of the Rings* be without the final scene of the ring falling into the fires of Mt. Doom? Imagine someone turning off the movie just before this critical scene because they felt the story was too dark and depressing. Just as you cannot reject a movie as being absurd when you only started watching it in the middle (and thus need to understand the backstory) so also, you cannot judge a movie's true worth if you turn it off before the big plot twist occurs near the end.

Those who accuse God of being unjust for ordering the violent destruction of the Canaanites do not interact with the backstory of God's patience and his justice, as well as the sin of the Canaanites, which brought about their destruction. Neither do they follow the story through to the end of the Bible. The result is an inaccurate portrayal of God's character (like someone accusing the good wizard Gandalf of being a villain because the only scene in *The Lord of the Rings* he or she watched was the time Gandalf "attacked" King Theoden in his throne room).[1]

In order to rightly understand God's character, this chapter will trace the Bible's themes of God's patience and justice with humanity to the big twist in the Bible's plotline.

THE BIG PICTURE - FUTURE JUDGEMENT

When we place the destruction of the Canaanites within the larger story of the Bible, we suddenly find (to our intense discomfort and distaste), that this ancient episode has direct relevance to our lives today. The Bible teaches that the judgments of God (like Noah's flood and the destruction of Sodom and Gomorrah) are previews of a future day of judgement that God will bring on the whole world. In this sense, the Canaanites are a representative picture of all humanity, both ancient and modern, living in rebellion against God.

As the Canaanites were idolatrous in turning away from God to serve gods of their own making, so the Bible asserts that all humanity has "exchanged the truth of God for a lie, and worshiped and served created things rather than the Creator— who is forever praised."[2] The supreme deity many people worship today is the god of self, as people decide for themselves how they will live.

Just as God was extremely patient with the Canaanites, so the Bible teaches that God has delayed the future day of judgement for thousands of years because "the Lord...is patient with you,

---

[1] King Theoden's mind was seduced by, and enslaved to, dark powers. Gandalf attacked him in order to free him.

[2] Romans 1:25.

not wanting anyone to perish, but everyone to come to repentance."[3]

And, just as a day finally came when justice required the judgement of the Canaanites, so the Bible says a day is coming when God will send Jesus to judge the whole earth for "God has set a day when he will judge the world with justice by the man he has appointed."[4]

Furthermore, just as the armies of Israel invaded Canaan, so the Bible declares a day is coming when the armies of heaven will invade the earth. Joshua led the armies of Israel; the armies of heaven will be led by a 'greater Joshua' (Jesus' name is the Greek translation of the Hebrew name Joshua.) Lastly, just as Joshua destroyed the Canaanites who refused to turn from their wrongdoing, so the Bible says Jesus will destroy all those who persist in rebellion against the King of the universe.

> I saw heaven standing open and there before me was a white horse, whose rider is called Faithful and True. With justice he judges and makes war…The armies of heaven were following him, riding on white horses and dressed in fine linen, white and clean. Out of his mouth comes a sharp sword with which to strike down the nations. "He will rule them with an iron scepter." He treads the winepress of the fury of the wrath of God Almighty. On his robe and on his thigh he has this name written: KING OF KINGS AND LORD OF LORDS.[5]

One further comparison between the Canaanites' day and ours: Rahab, a woman who lived in Jericho, described the Canaanites as "melting in fear"[6] before Israel's God. In the book of

---

[3] 2 Peter 3:9.
[4] Acts 17:31.
[5] Revelation 19:11-16.
[6] Joshua 2:11.

Revelation, we read the following description of that future day when Jesus returns:

> Then the kings of the earth, the princes, the generals, the rich, the mighty, and every slave and every free man hid in caves and among the rocks of the mountains. They called to the mountains and the rocks, "Fall on us and hide us from the face of him who sits on the throne and from the wrath of the Lamb! For the great day of their wrath has come, and who can stand?"[7]

There are few things more offensive to people of today than the idea that we are guilty of wrongdoing and therefore will some day be judged. Perhaps the Canaanites deserved it but surely we do not deserve God's punishment. After all, the argument goes, we are not like them. Or are we?

Like the Canaanites, have we not turned away from our Creator who gives us life and breath and everything else, in order to follow our own desires and be our own gods? Like the Canaanites, are we not a culture that rejects God's rules on sexuality as we experiment with and pursue every conceivable type of sexual gratification? Like the Canaanites, do we not enjoy entertainment that glorifies extreme violence, horror, murder, and bloodshed? Like the Canaanites, do we not sacrifice our children? It may not be to Molech, but do we not sacrifice our unborn children by the millions to the gods of

---

[7] Revelation 6:15-17.

career, a woman's choice, our own convenience, or the gender bias that values boys more than girls?[8]

We all want a God who is just but it is precisely the justice of God that is our great problem. After all, if we are guilty of wrongdoing, it means we, like the Canaanites, will eventually face judgment. Who can stand before such a just God?

THE TWIST IN THE PLOT

It is right here, at the point when the Bible's message is most dark, that the big twist in the plot occurs. The message of the Bible is that, despite our wrongdoing, God's heart is for, not against, his creation. The entire story of the Bible is the story of how God has worked out a way to rescue people from his own wrath. For God promised Abraham, "all peoples on earth will be blessed through you."[9] The big twist in the Bible's plotline is this: God has prepared a way to be just *and* to forgive us for

---

[8] "In 2010, the latest year on record, 64,641 abortions were performed on Canadian women as reported by hospitals and clinics. According to The Canadian Institute for Health Information (CIHI), who have taken over the role of disseminating abortion data from Statistics Canada, this number does not include abortions performed in Quebec, clinic data for British Columbia is incomplete due to voluntary reporting, and abortions performed on women who reside outside Ontario but who have received an abortion in an Ontario clinic are not included, meaning that the actual figure, while unknown, is much higher.

Even with underreported and underrepresented figures, it is clear that more than three million abortions have occurred in Canada since 1969, when abortion was first decriminalized. Statistics Canada tables show a recorded total of 2,838,328 abortions between 1974 and 2006. CIHI tables show a recorded total of 353,034 abortions between 2007 and 2010, which means that the total number of 'reported' abortions that took place between 1974 and 2010 in Canada is 3,191,362." http://abortionincanada.ca/stats /annual-abortion-rates/ (accessed May 10, 2015).

[9] Genesis 12:3.

our wrongdoing, which means we can escape the punishment we deserve.

This solution to the punishment and violence of God begins with a plan God made before he created the world. In eternity past God planned to send his Son into the world in order that he might take the punishment we deserve upon himself. This is why the Bible says, "[Jesus] was chosen before the creation of the world" and that he is "the Lamb that was slain from the creation of the world."[10] We must not, however, think that Jesus was forced to follow God's plan that led to his violent death. Jesus repeatedly stated that when he laid down his life it would be done willingly: "No one takes [my life] from me, but I lay it down of my own accord. I have authority to lay it down and authority to take it up again."[11] In other words, the Son voluntarily accepted the mission assigned to him by his Father. On the cross, Jesus, the one man in history who did not deserve judgement, took upon himself the punishment we deserved that we might have peace with God: "...he was pierced for our transgressions, he was crushed for our iniquities, the punishment that brought us peace was upon him and by his wounds we are healed."[12]

At the heart of the cross is what theologians call "penal substitution." The word "penal" is a legal term that speaks of paying a penalty. Jesus' death on the cross is, therefore, to be understood, in part, as a punishment.[13] A "substitute" is someone who does something on behalf of another. Penal substitution is a shorthand way of describing the Bible's

---

[10] 1 Peter 1:20; Revelation 13:8.

[11] John 10:18.

[12] Isaiah 53:5.

[13] It is also to be understood in other ways such as Christ's victory of evil: "And having disarmed the powers and authorities, he made a public spectacle of them, triumphing over them by the cross" (Colossians 2:15).

teaching that on the cross Jesus voluntarily acted as our substitute by taking upon himself the punishment we deserved for our wickedness.

A BURNT PATCH OF GROUND

In pioneer days families living on prairie lands would sometimes find themselves about to be burned alive. A family might walk out of their house and see a great plume of black smoke in the distance. They knew the wind was whipping up a prairie fire and pushing it toward their homestead. Prairie fires burn hot and fast reaching seven hundred degrees Fahrenheit, travelling at speeds of six hundred feet per minute. There was only one hope for families in such a situation: they would run into the middle of the field and set their own livelihood on fire. As their crops were consumed, a large patch of burnt ground would form and the entire family would stand in the middle of it. The fire would race toward them, but would suddenly stop at the edge of the burnt ground. The fire would turn aside to the left and the right, but it would not engulf the family because the ground on which they stood had already been burnt.

The Bible presents Jesus Christ as the "burnt patch of ground for sinners". Since God's wrath burned against Jesus, those who stand in him will be escape the future judgement of God for "[Jesus] rescues us from the coming wrath."[14] It is because Jesus is this safe patch of burnt ground that the Bible calls people to entrust themselves to him: "whoever believes in the Son has eternal life, but whoever rejects the Son will not see life, for God's wrath remains on him."[15]

---

[14] 1 Thessalonians 1:10.
[15] John 3:36.

The grand story of the Bible is a celebration of what God has done to rescue sinners through the violent death of Jesus Christ. Over and over, the biblical writers revel in and exult over this good news: "Since we have now been justified by his blood, how much more shall we be saved from God's wrath through him" and "There is now no condemnation for those who are in Christ Jesus."[16] It is Bible verses like these that have led Christians to write songs expressing the Bible's solution to the violence of God.

- Bearing shame and scoffing rude,
  In my place condemned he stood;
  Sealed my pardon with his blood.
  Hallelujah! What a Saviour.[17]

- Because the sinless Saviour died,
  My sinful soul is counted free;
  For God the just is satisfied,
  To look on Him and pardon me.[18]

- And I beheld God's love displayed,
  You suffered in my place.
  You bore the wrath reserved for me,
  Now all I know is grace.[19]

- Amazing love, How can it be,
  That Thou my God shouldst die for me.[20]

---

[16] Romans 5:9; 8:1.
[17] Lyrics from *Hallelujah, What a Savior!* by Philip P. Bliss.
[18] Lyrics from *Before The Throne of God Above* by Charitie Lees Bancroft. Originally titled *Advocate*.
[19] Lyrics from *All I Have Is Christ* by Jordan Kauflin.
[20] Lyrics from *And Can It Be?* by Charles Wesley.

CONCLUSION

The past few chapters have sought to argue that God is not an evil monster who should be rejected because of his unjust character. To the contrary, God's character is shown to be morally upright in that he was patient with the Canaanites and did not punish them for just one wrong act or even one hundred years of wickedness.

God's character is also shown to be just in that he does not let wrongdoing continue forever. Rather, he is a God who cares about good and evil. Just as we patiently seek to rehabilitate criminals but will eventually bring strict justice upon those who stubbornly persist in wrongdoing, so God eventually brought justice upon the Canaanites.

Subsequently, we may accept that the Canaanites deserved this punishment and we begin to applaud God's just character. Our applause quickly turns to silence, however, and then to cries of "Unfair!" when the Bible says that, like the Canaanites, we are also deserving of judgement.

However, the Bible's story is not about God seeking to destroy humanity. Rather, it is the story of how God, in grace and love, has found a way to be just and to forgive people. Out of love, God sent his Son Jesus into this world to bear himself the punishment that we deserve in order that God's justice might be satisfied, that we might be forgiven and reconciled to God.

PROBLEM #4:
EXCLUSIVITY & INTOLERANCE

HOW CAN THERE POSSIBLY BE ONLY ONE WAY TO GOD?

INTRODUCTION

To many people living in our pluralistic culture, the problem with Christianity can be summed up in one word: exclusivity. How can Christians say Jesus is the only way to God? Such exclusivity is distasteful to many people because it comes across as arrogant and intolerant.

When people raise this question, it is usually expressed something like this: "How can Christians *possibly* believe there is only one path to God?" Or, "Are you *seriously* telling me Christians are right and others are wrong?" Within these questions, and the tone that usually accompanies them, is the feeling that it is arrogant to believe there is only one, exclusive way to God.

Charles Templeton, who preached alongside Billy Graham but later became an atheist, writes in *Farewell to God*,

> It is insufferable presumption for the Bible to claim that besides Jesus there is no other name under heaven by which we must be saved…Christians are a small minority in the world.
> Approximately four out of every five people on the face of the earth believe in gods other than the Christian God…Are we to believe that only Christians are right?[1]

On one of her shows, Oprah Winfrey engaged in a heated discussion with some women about the idea of Jesus being the only way to God. She summarized well the incredulity that people feel toward a belief that is so exclusive: "There are millions of ways to be a human being and many paths to what

---

[1] Charles Templeton, *Farewell to God* (Toronto: McClelland & Stewart, 2011), 27.

you call 'God.' Her path might be something else and when she gets there she might call it 'the Light'...there couldn't possibly be just one way."[2]

In addition to being viewed as arrogant, it is also believed that Christianity's teaching on the exclusivity of Christ leads to intolerance on many levels, including violence. It does not take long for a critic of Christianity to bring up the Crusades, the Salem witch trials, African-American slavery, and the discriminatory behaviors of many Christians toward the LGBTQ community. When these examples are placed alongside other perpetrators of religious violence such as ISIS, Al Qaeda, Hamas, as well as the Sunni-Shiite conflicts, it seems hard to escape the conclusion that religion is one of the greatest obstacles to tolerance and world peace.

How can Christians possibly hold such exclusive views on Jesus when we live in a world of diverse beliefs that so desperately needs peace? This is the subject of the next three chapters.

---

[2] *The Oprah Winfrey Show*, 2/15/2007. https://www.youtube.com/watch?v=noO_dCWtB1E

Chapter 13
The Exclusive Claim That Jesus Makes

Do not let your hearts be troubled. Trust in God; trust also in me. In my Father's house are many rooms; if it were not so, I would have told you. I am going there to prepare a place for you. And if I go and prepare a place for you, I will come back and take you to be with me that you also may be where I am. You know the way to the place where I am going." Thomas said to him, "Lord, we don't know where you are going, so how can we know the way?" Jesus answered, "I am the way and the truth and the life. No one comes to the Father except through me.[1]

- Jesus

"Seek first to understand, then seek to be understood."[2] This axiom of interpersonal communication is particularly important when there is disagreement. Far too often we respond in quick debate only to realize later in the discussion that we lacked a complete picture and thus gave a misdirected response.

---

[1] John 14:1-6.
[2] Stephen Covey, *The 7 Habits of Highly Effective People: Powerful Lessons in Personal Change 25th Anniversary Edition* (RosettaBooks, 2013), Kindle Edition, Location 4141.

Whether we agree with the Christian claim of Jesus being the only way to God or not, it is important to understand *what* Jesus claims and *why* he claims it before we reject it. In this chapter, I will clarify the exclusive claim Jesus makes and demonstrate how it fits into the larger story of the Bible.

CLARIFYING JESUS' CLAIM

When people look at Jesus' life they typically agree that he was an incredibly humble man. He was approachable, tender, others-focused, and caring toward people the society of his day looked down on, like the poor and prostitutes. It is Jesus' humility that leads many people, like Gandhi, Bono, and Queen Elizabeth, to admire and revere him. *TIME* magazine went so far as to assert, "the single most powerful figure – not merely in these two millenniums [sic] but in all human history – has been Jesus of Nazareth...a serious argument can be made that no one else's life has proved remotely as powerful and enduring as that of Jesus."[3] There is no doubt that Jesus' humility is a major contributing factor to the enduring power of Jesus' life.

What is fascinating, though, is how Jesus would not allow people to simply admire him. He was always pushing the envelope on how he wanted people to think of him. One of the greatest examples of this is the claim Jesus made about himself in John 14:6: "I am the way and the truth and the life. No one comes to the Father except through me."

Note carefully that Jesus does *not* say, "I have come to *point the way* to God." Several founders of other religions have claimed this. Mohammed claimed to be a prophet who pointed the way to Allah. Joseph Smith, the founder of Mormonism, also claimed to be a prophet who points the way to God. Jesus,

---

[3] Reynolds Price, "Jesus of Nazareth", *Time Magazine*, November 28, 1999.

however, does not say he came to point the way to God. Rather, he says, *"I am* the way…no one comes to the Father except *through me."* In the original Greek in which this was written, it is stated more forcefully. Jesus literally says, "I, I am the way." The use of the "I" is akin to our modern practice of typing a word in bold and underlining it. Jesus says that it is not through following certain teachings or doing certain things that we can come to God the Father. Rather, the way is through *him.*

Notice also that Jesus does not say, "I am *a* way to God."[4] He does not say, "I am one way among many by which people may come to God the Father." That would still be a massive claim but Jesus goes much further. He says, "I am *the* way…no one comes to the Father *except* through me." Again, the original Greek uses the definite article, "the."

Before moving on, it is important to clarify that Jesus is not saying everything non-Christians believe is wrong. C.S. Lewis explains:

> If you are a Christian you do not have to believe that all the other religions are simply wrong all through…If you are a Christian, you are free to think that all these religions, even the queerest ones, contain at least some hint of the truth…But, of course, being a Christian does mean thinking that where Christianity differs from other religions, Christianity is right and they are wrong. As in arithmetic-there is only one right answer to a sum, and all other answers are wrong: but some of the wrong answers are much nearer being right than others.[5]

---

[4] The original Greek uses the definite article "the" and therefore has no confusion with "a."

[5] C.S. Lewis, *Mere Christianity* (New York: HarperCollins e-books, 2009), Kindle Edition, Location 598.

In summary, Jesus claims he is the only way by which people may come to God the Father. This is, without doubt, a very exclusive claim.

JESUS' CLAIM WITHIN THE BIBLE'S STORY

To properly understand Jesus' claim (whether we agree with it or not) we must see how it fits within the Bible's big story. The Bible's larger story asserts that, although God is our Creator, and the one who gives us all good things, we have all turned away from our Creator in order to live for ourselves. The Bible calls this "sin" and declares that sin separates us from God. Rather than destroy the rebellious human race, the Bible teaches that, from the moment of our first rebellion, God has been working out a way to bring us back to himself; a plan that originated "before the creation of the world."[6] Jesus claims to be *the* way because he alone can deal with and forgive the sin that has alienated us from God. This story reaches a climax at the cross where Jesus took the punishment we deserve for our sins so that all who receive him are reconciled to God.

Jesus claims to be the only way to God because he claims to be the only one who can deal with our sin. This is an extremely

---

[6] Ephesians 1:4. The entire verse says, "For he chose us in him before the creation of the world to be holy and blameless in his sight." The Bible describes the salvation of God's people through the death of Jesus as accomplished in history but planned by God before he created the universe. This is why Jesus' death can be described as being planned and, in a sense, accomplished before creation: "He was chosen before the creation of the world, but was revealed in these last times for your sake" (1 Peter 1:20); "...whose names have not been written in the book of life belonging to the Lamb that was slain from the creation of the world" (Revelation 13:8); "Indeed Herod and Pontius Pilate met together with the Gentiles and the people of Israel in this city to conspire against your holy servant Jesus, whom you anointed. They did what your power and will had decided beforehand should happen" (Acts 4:27-28).

unique claim in the history of the world. If we asked Mohammed to forgive our sins he would tear his robes and say, "Blasphemy! I cannot do such a thing." Joseph Smith and Moses would say the same thing. If we asked a Hindu priest about the possibility of having our sins removed he would say, "Impossible! The law of karma will give you what you deserve."

> If all we need is a teacher of enlightenment, the Buddha will do; if all we need is a collection of gods for every occasion and need and hope, Hinduism will do; if all we need is a tribal deity, any tribal deity will do; if all we need is a lawgiver, Moses will do; if all we need is a set of rules and a way of devotion, Muhammad or Joseph Smith will do; if all we need is inspiration and insight into the sovereign self, Oprah will do; but if we need a savior, only Jesus will do.[7]

MOUNTAIN PATH OR MAZE?

People often speak about God as the top of a mountain. Religion and spirituality are then portrayed as the many different paths that lead to the top of the mountain. The point of the image is to say that, in the end, all paths make it to the top (to God) and therefore no one path can be called *the* path. Yet Jesus' claim requires us to ask if the paths are more like a maze than a simple trail up a mountain? What if humanity is lost in a giant maze? There are many paths to follow in a maze but there is only one path that ultimately gets a person out of a maze. Jesus is claiming that he is *the* path that will lead us out of the maze and into the presence of God the Father.[8]

---

[7] Albert Mohler speaking at the 2014 T4G Conference. http://news.sbts.edu/2014/04/24/mohler-at-t4g-conference-on-evangelism-exclusivity-makes-the-gospel-more-beautiful/ (accessed May 10, 2015)
[8] Michael Green, *But Don't All Religions Lead to God?: Navigating the Multi-Faith Maze* (Grand Rapids: Baker Books, 2002), Kindle Edition, Location 258.

So far we have simply tried to clarify Jesus' exclusive claim. At the end of the day, however, this exclusivity is precisely what people find to be arrogant and intolerant. Before we accept this conclusion, let's consider the exclusive claims of other religions (chapter 14) and of secularism (chapter 15).

Chapter 14
The Exclusive Claims That Religions Make

In this chapter I aim to show that 1) Jesus' exclusive claim is not nearly as arrogant as we may think because all religions make exclusive claims and 2) all religious claims can lead to intolerance and even violence.

ALL WORLD RELIGIONS MAKE EXCLUSIVE CLAIMS

We need to understand that all world religions, not just Christianity, make exclusive claims. This may strike us as odd because we often hear that the world's religions believe essentially the same thing. This is a very attractive idea; if all views are basically the same, then all views are equally valid. The problem is that the religions themselves do not believe they are the same as each other. They may be superficially the same but they are fundamentally different.

Take the basic question of who or what God, Allah, Ultimate Reality, the Supreme Being, or the Divine is. (We can already start to see the differences when we cannot even agree on a term. For consistency, I will use "the Divine"). Aside from Buddhism, every world religion agrees that the Divine exists. On this point, most world religions are superficially the same. However, every religion makes exclusive claims about the Divine that directly contradict each other and therefore end up being fundamentally different.

In Hinduism, the Divine is an impersonal ultimate reality called Brahman that is manifested through many gods and goddesses. Hindus believe the spirits of these gods and goddesses fill, or can fill, the statues that depict them. Worship before a statue is, therefore, a key part of Hinduism. In direct contradiction to this, Judaism says there is only one God who is a personal being, and this personal God absolutely prohibits the making of statues (idols) for use in worship.

Christians believe Jesus is the eternal Son of God and therefore should be worshipped as God. Islam rejects this and emphatically declares that God has no Son.

In Hinduism, there is no forgiveness from an impersonal ultimate reality. There is only the ruthless law of karma that says, "you sin, you pay." In direct contrast to this, Christianity says you can have your sins forgiven because Jesus says, "You sin, I pay."[1]

Reflecting on the commonly held idea that all religions are essentially the same, the Indian-born writer Ravi Zacharias writes:

> All religions are not the same...At the heart of every religion is
> an uncompromising commitment to a particular way of defining

---

[1] Michael Green, *But Don't All Religions Lead to God?*, Kindle Edition, Location 258.

who God is or is not and accordingly, of defining life's purpose. Anyone who claims that all religions are the same betrays not only an ignorance of religions but also a caricatured view of even the best known ones. Every religion at its core is exclusive.[2]

The Dalai Lama agrees. In his book *Kindness, Clarity, and Insight* he writes, "Among spiritual faiths, there are many different philosophies, some just opposite to each other on certain points. Buddhists do not accept a creator; Christians base their philosophy on that theory."[3]

So we see it is not just Jesus who makes exclusive claims. Every religion does. Ironically, the one thing on which all religions agree is that they are different from each other.

The point here should be clear by now: all world religions make exclusive claims.

RELIGIOUS INTOLERANCE AND VIOLENCE

There is no question that the exclusive claims of the world's religions can lead to arrogance and intolerance. Religious people can act like they are the "good" people who are in with God while looking down their noses at the "bad" non-religious people who ignore God. Furthermore, religious people can act condescendingly toward the "bad" religious people who, in their view, do not worship God the way they believe he should be worshipped. This exclusivity can quickly turn to intolerance and even violence.

---

[2] Ravi Zacharias, *Jesus Among Other Gods* (Nashville: W Publishing Group, 2000), 7.
[3] The Dalai Lama, *Kindness, Clarity, and Insight* (Snow Lion, 2013), 45.

Christopher Hitchens devotes an entire chapter of *god Is Not Great* to chronicling and rebuking the violent intolerance of religion. Titling this chapter "Religion Kills," Hitchens argues that religious exclusivity is at the heart of intolerance because religion heightens and intensifies the differences between people: "Religion is not unlike racism. One version of it inspires and provokes the other...Religion has been an enormous multiplier of suspicion and hatred, with members of each group talking of the other in precisely the tones of a bigot."[4] Hitchens' book contains one story after another of religious intolerance and violence.

Richard Dawkins also devotes much of *The God Delusion* to arguing the case that religion causes violence. Ridding the world of religion, Dawkins believes, would remove one of the greatest threats to world peace.

John Lennon cast the same vision in his song *Imagine*:

> Imagine there's no heaven
> It's easy if you try
> No hell below us
> Above us only sky
> Imagine all the people
> Living for today...
>
> Imagine there's no countries
> It isn't hard to do
> Nothing to kill or die for
> And no religion too
> Imagine all the people
> Living life in peace...
>
> You may say I'm a dreamer

---

4 Hitchens, *god Is Not Great*, 35-36.

But I'm not the only one
I hope someday you'll join us
And the world will be as one[5]

THE SLIPPERY SLOPE OF RELIGION

It may surprise you to read that I, a Christian pastor, largely agree that religion easily leads to intolerance and even violence. I resonate with Dr. Timothy Keller when he writes,

> Religion, generally speaking, tends to create a slippery slope in the human heart. Each religion informs its followers that they have "the truth," and this naturally leads them to feel superior to those with differing beliefs. Also, a religion tells its followers that they are saved and connected to God by devotedly performing that truth. This moves them to separate from those who are less devoted and pure in life. Therefore, it is easy for one religious group to stereotype and caricature other ones. Once this situation exists it can easily spiral down into the marginalization of others or even to active oppression, abuse, or violence against them.[6]

The discussion so far has led us to acknowledge two conclusions: first, all religions make exclusive claims; second, all religious claims can tend toward arrogance and intolerance.

IS GETTING RID OF RELIGION THE ANSWER?

In light of this, many people say, "This is exactly why I am secular and not religious. Religion is too exclusive and arrogant

---

[5] John Lennon, *Imagine*, on Imagine (Apple Records, 1971).
[6] Timothy Keller, *The Reason for God: Belief in an Age of Skepticism* (New York: Dutton, 2008), 4.

and often leads to violence. How ridiculous to think one religion has a corner on God or that one religion is right while all the others are wrong." But is secularism any different? Would the world be largely freed of intolerance and violence if we all embraced the vision of a world without religion? This is the topic of the next chapter.

Chapter 15
The Exclusive Claims That Secular People Make

"Secular but spiritual."[1] This is how one West coast author describes people in my home province of British Columbia, Canada. In our nation, British Columbia ranks highest in terms of people who say they have no religion. This does not mean, however, that we have no interest in spiritual things. It is simply that there is a major distinction in people's minds between spirituality and organized religion.

One of the primary reasons for this aversion to organized religion is our cultural ethos that says, "What's true for me does not necessarily have to be true for you." In fact, very often the unforgivable sin in Canadian culture is to suggest your view is right and someone else's view is wrong. Since religions make

[1] Douglas Todd ed., *Cascadia: The Elusive Utopia – Exploring the Spirit of the Pacific Northwest* (Vancouver: Ronsdale Press, 2008), 12.

exclusive claims about what is right and wrong, they are rejected as narrow, intolerant, dogmatic, and even bigoted. The problem with this way of thinking is that it fails to recognize the basic fact that secular people (not just religious people) also make exclusive claims.[2]

ELEPHANTS AND SECULAR ARROGANCE

At this point in a discussion on God and religion, many secular people will raise the parable of the blind men and the elephant. A king brings in some blind men and has them touch certain parts of the elephant. One man feels the trunk and says, "It's a tree." Another feels the tail and says, "It's a rope." Since they are blind, each one has a different explanation. The wise king, however, can see the truth – that they are all touching the same elephant. Using this as an allegory, the secular person says the blind men are world religions and the elephant is God. There is an obvious point to this parable: religious people need to stop being so arrogant in thinking their exclusive claims about God are correct because each only possesses a part of the whole truth.

Again, this sounds very attractive, but many people fail to recognize how arrogant this story actually is. Ask yourself this question: who is the secular person claiming to be in the parable? The secular person is claiming to be the wise king who alone can see what the religious people cannot. The secular person is claiming to be able take an objective viewpoint on all of reality and to possess enlightened knowledge that religious people blindly ignore. For this reason, we often find secular people, particularly the new atheists, looking down their noses and ridiculing the poor religious people who just don't get it. It is fair to ask, however, who gave secular people such an

---

[2] I am using the word "secular" in the basic sense of non-religious.

enlightened viewpoint? Why should we assume secular people can see the truth of religion better than the religious people themselves? If we are going to use this parable, humility would require us to interpret the blind men as representing the efforts of all people (both religious and secular) as they try to make sense of their experience.

We need to press further into this idea that secular people, like religious people, always make exclusive claims. For instance, it is common to hear a secular person say, "I don't believe in the God of religion. I believe in a God who is tolerant, all loving, and does not judge people for who they sleep with or what they do." This claim is just as exclusive as any religious claim for the person is claiming to know what God is like. Moreover, it is also quite arrogant; where do people get such lofty knowledge about the nature of God? At least religions like Judaism, Islam, and Christianity have the humility to say they only know what God is like because God has chosen to reveal himself (they believe the elephant has spoken and therefore ignorant humanity can understand what he is like). Ironically, the secular person is claiming that his or her finite mind, which even lacks understanding as to how the opposite sex works, has the ability to understand the nature and character of the Divine. Finally, this secular claim about a non-judgemental God ends up excluding the billions of people who do believe God *will* hold us accountable for how we live. Simply put, the secular person has developed his or her own exclusive view of God.

THE MOST EXCLUSIVE SECULAR CLAIM

After considering all that has been said in this chapter, many other secular people end up saying, "Well I just don't believe absolute truth exists at all. I don't believe there is one truth that everyone must believe. People can believe whatever they want, as long as they don't hurt each other."

Again this sounds very humble, and even noble, but such a statement is one of the biggest, most exclusive, inconsistent, and culturally narrow claims a person can make. It is a very big claim because the person is saying, "the one true thing in the universe I know for sure is that there is no truth." It is inconsistent because, in a right desire to forbid things like rape, the person then says there is at least one absolute truth everyone must follow, namely, that we not hurt each other. But if there is at least one absolute truth everyone must follow then why can't there be more? Furthermore, this claim is extremely exclusive because the person is saying, "Anyone who does believe in absolute truth is *wrong*." Finally, it is culturally narrow because virtually everyone in the history of the world, and the vast majority of people alive today, believe absolute truth exists. Try asserting the idea that there is no such thing as absolute truth in India, Africa, or the Middle East and see how people respond. We see, then, that the supposed inclusivity of this claim ends up being so drastically exclusive that it rejects almost every person alive on the planet today and the vast majority of people in history.

It all comes down to this one point: we are all exclusivists. It is impossible not to be. Every time we claim something is true, we are, by definition, claiming that its opposite is false.

SECULAR INTOLERANCE AND VIOLENCE

Secular exclusivity, like religious exclusivity, also creates a slippery slope in people's hearts, which can lead to intolerance and even violence. Religious people can think of themselves as the "good" people and look down their noses at the "bad" secular people. But secular people can think of themselves as the enlightened ones who understand what those ignorant religious people don't get. Secular people can then become very intolerant of religious people and also of secular people with whom they disagree.

When society rejects God as its ultimate ideal, it will simply fill the void with another ultimate ideal that it feels is superior to God. This new idea then becomes the new exclusive standard and anyone who disagrees will be discriminated against and even suppressed. It was in the name of socialism that Pol Pot killed his millions in Cambodia. The Nazis justified the Holocaust on the basis of racial purity. The French Revolution discarded all notions of God and elevated the concept of liberty to the ultimate place. When people disagreed with how liberty should be practised, they were killed. Recall the famous incident in 1793 when Madame Roland, a revolutionary herself, went to the guillotine on trumped up charges because she fell out of favour with the revolutionary elite. She bowed to the statue personifying liberty and said, "Liberty, what crimes are committed in your name." As one must acknowledge, religion can lead to violence but it is false to say religion is *the* cause of intolerance and violence, because history shows that *any* ultimate ideal can be abused.[3]

What if John Lennon's dream came true and we managed to rid the world of religion? Would a society built purely on secular values result in world peace? The history of the 20th century reveals this to be a naïve dream that turned into a nightmare. Think only of the big three atheistic or secular regimes of the 20th century: Communist Russia, Communist China, and Nazi Germany. Stalin was responsible for about 20 million deaths. Jung Chang and Jon Halliday's recent study *Mao: The Unknown Story* attributes about 70 million deaths to Mao Zedong's

---

[3] This paragraph inspired by Alistair McGrath in Zacharias ed. *Beyond Opinion*, 28-31 and Keller, *The Reason for God*, 55-56.

regime. Hitler comes in third with around 10 million murders.[4] Alistair McGrath writes, "The 20th century gave rise to one of the greatest and most distressing paradoxes of human history: that the greatest intolerance and violence of that century were practised by those who believed that religion causes intolerance and violence."[5] It is clear then that *all* ideals, whether religious or secular, can quickly lead to intolerance and violence.[6]

Is there any way out of this dilemma? This is the subject of the next chapter.

---

[4] Dinesh D'Souza, *What's So Great About Christianity?* (Washington: Regnery Publishing, Inc., 2007), 214.

[5] Alister McGrath, *The Twilight of Atheism: The Rise and Fall of Disbelief in the Modern World* (Oxford University Press, 2004), 230.

[6] For further discussion see, McGrath, *The Dawkins Delusion*, 75-99; Keller, *The Reason for God*, 51-67; D'Souza, *What's So Great About Christianity?*, 203-224.

Chapter 16
The Exclusive Claim That Makes Us Humble

In *The Great Divorce* C.S. Lewis gives a fictional account of hell. When the main character arrives, he finds a city of empty houses. It is explained to him that newcomers move into these houses but within twenty-four hours are quarrelling with their neighbours. Before the week is over, the argument has escalated to such a high level of hostility that the neighbours move apart. This process keeps happening so that each person in hell moves further and further away from each other. The main character asks another man where the people who had arrived thousands of years ago have gone.

> They've been moving on and on. Getting further apart. They're so far off by now…astronomical distances. There's a bit of rising ground near where I live and a chap has a telescope. You can see the lights of the inhabited houses, where those old ones

live, millions of miles away. Millions of miles from us and from one another.[1]

The man then mentions Napoleon, one of the closer ones.

> Two men went to see him. It took about fifteen thousand years to get to his house. When they got there they saw Napoleon pacing back and forth in his house always muttering to himself, "It was Soult's fault. It was Ney's fault. It was Josephine's fault. It was the fault of the Russians. It was the fault of the English."[2]

Lewis has captured the inherent pride of our hearts - a pride that holds our own exclusive viewpoints so strongly that we become intolerant and hostile toward those who disagree with us. Is there any way out of this dilemma? There does not seem to be; as we have seen, we are all exclusivists. We are all, therefore, prone to the pride that results from holding an exclusive position, as well as the slippery slope of our hearts that treats those who disagree with us with intolerance, even violence.

TAKING JESUS TOO SERIOUSLY?

The question now becomes this: *Is there any exclusive belief system that can work against the slippery slope of our hearts and produce a humility that treats others with genuine love and respect?* In this chapter, I want to show how Jesus' exclusive claim, when understood rightly and applied deeply, has the power to generate this humility, even toward people who are hostile to us.

In saying that Christianity has the power to generate this humility, I am not in any way trying to minimize or justify the

---

1 C.S. Lewis, *The Great Divorce* (New York: Simon & Schuster, 1996), 20.
2 Lewis, *The Great Divorce*, 22.

actions of Christians who have acted arrogantly or even violently. These attitudes and behaviours must be admitted and confronted. My point in this chapter is that such arrogance and violence is not the result of taking Jesus' exclusive claim too seriously. Rather, it is the result of not taking Jesus' claim seriously enough.

THE POWER OF GRACE

Christianity has the power to smash pride and to generate humility in our hearts because its core message is one of grace. Jesus' exclusive claim is an assault on human pride because it says our goodness is not good enough to get us to God. Yet it also generates profound humility, for it declares that God will accept us on the goodness of another – Jesus Christ. The Bible calls this unmerited and undeserved gift "grace." What we cannot do for ourselves, God does for us in Jesus. What we do not deserve, and cannot earn, God gives as a gift.

The message of Christianity is not, "go to church, obey God's commands, clean up your life, and then God will accept you." If this were the message, there would be grounds for pride, because Christians could look down on all those who do not obey as they do. The message is not "obey and God will accept you" but rather "admit your disobedience and trust Jesus to make you right with God."

When people take Jesus and his exclusive claim seriously they can no longer think of themselves as better than others. The cross declares that our sin was so bad that nothing less than the death of God's Son could remedy it. They can no longer smugly feel that they are smarter than everyone else because they have discovered that, apart from the grace of God, they would still be lost in their sin. Furthermore, they can no longer act in violence toward their enemies. Their Lord prayed for his enemies while they crucified him saying, "Father, forgive them for they do not know what they are doing," and they are called to follow in their Lord's steps.[3]

To be clear, what Christianity offers is not simply the command to love other people. It most certainly does this but, more importantly, it gives us the power we need to develop a humble heart that genuinely desires to follow this command. For instance, when the Christians in the ancient town of Philippi were at odds with each other, the apostle Paul wrote to them saying, "Do nothing out of selfish ambition or vain conceit, but in humility consider others better than yourselves. Each of you should look not only to your own interests, but also to the interests of others."[4] This command sounds wonderful, but when you are angry with someone else, where do you get the humility that is necessary to carry it out? Answer: from going deeper into all that Jesus has done for you. Immediately following this command, Paul calls them to take Jesus more seriously by taking on his attitude:

> Your attitude should be the same as that of Christ Jesus: Who, being in very nature God, did not consider equality with God something to be grasped, but made himself nothing, taking the very nature of a servant, being made in human likeness. And being found in appearance as a man, he humbled himself and became obedient to death— even death on a cross![5]

In other words, Paul is saying, "The fact that you are still filled with pride, and are quarrelling with each other is evidence that you have not taken Jesus seriously enough. Jesus humbled himself by giving up his rights as God and becoming a man. He further humbled himself in serving his own creation and, in the

---

[3] Luke 23:34.
[4] Philippians 2:3-4.
[5] Philippians 2:5-11.

supreme act of looking to the interests of others, he gave his life for us on the cross."

HOW GRACE TRANSFORMS
PRIDE AND INTOLERANCE

The transforming power of grace is one of the great themes in *Les Miserables*. Jean Valjean, the bitter and hardened ex-convict steals some silver plates from a bishop who had kindly taken him into his house. He is caught by the police and brought back to the bishop's home. Valjean expects to be locked up for the rest of his days but in an act of grace the Bishop rushes up to him and says:

> "Ah there you are!…I am glad so see you. But! I gave you the candlesticks also, which are silver like the rest, and would bring two hundred francs. Why did you not take them along with your plates?" Jean Valjean opened his eyes and looked at the bishop with an expression which no human tongue could describe.[6]

The proud Valjean is so stunned by the bishop's undeserved kindness that he cannot believe he is free to go: " 'Is it true that they let me go?' he said in a voice almost inarticulate, as if he were speaking in his sleep."[7] The bishop's act of grace sends him reeling: "Jean Valjean was trembling in every limb. He took the two candlesticks mechanically, and with a wild appearance…[he] felt like a man who is just about to faint."[8] The bishop then says:

---

[6] Victor Hugo, *Les Miserables*, trans. Charles E Wilbour (New York: Everyman's Library Alfred A. Knopf, 1998), 111.
[7] Hugo, *Les Miserables*, 111.
[8] Hugo, *Les Miserables*, 111-112.

"Forget not, never forget that you have promised me to use this silver to become an honest man…Jean Valjean, my brother: you belong no longer to evil, but to good. It is your soul that I am buying for you. I withdraw it from dark thoughts and from the spirit of perdition, and I give it to God!"[9]

Valjean's pride had never broken under the harsh treatment he endured in prison, yet this single act of grace shattered him.

To this celestial tenderness, he opposed pride, which is the fortress of evil in man. He felt dimly that the pardon of this priest was the hardest insult, and the most formidable attack which he had yet sustained…like an owl who should see the sun suddenly rise, the convict had been dazzled and blinded by virtue. *One thing was certain, nor did he himself doubt it, that he was no longer the same man, that all was changed in him.*[10]

With his pride crushed, the bishop's unmerited gift created a new spirit of kindness within the soul of Valjean. He extends mercy to the orphaned child Cosette and raises her as his own. He improves the socio-economic state of an entire town. Perhaps most powerfully, he forgives the policeman Javert who has relentlessly pursued him and tried to destroy his life. All of this kindness toward others is the direct result of his personal and profound experience of grace. Valjean keeps the candlesticks as tangible symbols of the grace that transformed his life. They remain on his mantel and on his deathbed he leaves them to his daughter saying, "To her I bequeath the two candlesticks which are on the mantel. They are silver; but to me they are gold, they are diamond."[11]

---

[9] Hugo, *Les Miserables*, 112.

[10] Hugo, *Les Miserables*, 116-117. Emphasis mine.

[11] Hugo, *Les Miserables*, 1430.

CONCLUSION

There is no question that Jesus' claim is exclusive. Like the path that leads out of a maze, Jesus claims that he is the only way lost people can find their way back to God. The larger story of the Bible is the key to making sense of this claim. If all people are sinners, and Jesus is the only one who can truly deal with our sin, then it makes sense that he is the only way to God.

Although people find Jesus' claim to be arrogant, we have seen that all religions and all secular people also make exclusive claims. It is impossible not to be exclusive, for as soon as people state what they believe on any subject such as the character of God, they are, by definition, excluding any view that disagrees with their own.

Furthermore, although religious exclusivity can certainly lead to intolerance and violence, it is equally true that any ideal can be used to marginalize and oppress those who are in disagreement. History is filled with examples of religious and secular intolerance that, sadly, *has* often led to violence.

In this final chapter on *Exclusivity and Intolerance* I suggested that Christianity has the unique power to break the chains of arrogance and intolerance that bind the human heart and to generate a humility that treats other with love and respect. This is because, at its very core, the exclusive claims of Christianity are about the grace of God in Jesus Christ. When people see that they are not good enough to be accepted by God, but that Jesus has made us good enough, they can no longer think of themselves as better than anyone else. When they see how loving God has been toward them in Jesus (though they do not deserve it), it begins to change them at the very core of who they are so that they begin to treat others with grace. Christians can certainly act in arrogant and intolerant ways, but this is not because they are taking Jesus' exclusive claims too seriously. It is because they are not taking Jesus' claims seriously enough.

PROBLEM #5: GOD & EVIL

IF GOD IS GOOD, WHY IS THERE SO MUCH EVIL IN THE WORLD?

INTRODUCTION

If God is good, why is there so much evil in the world? This question is commonly referred to as "the problem of evil" and, for many people, the problem of evil is *the* problem with Christianity. The problem of evil states that if God is good and all-powerful then evil cannot exist. However, since we know evil exists, God is either not good (because he allows it) or he is not all-powerful (because he does not stop it.) The conclusion is that the existence of evil is incompatible with the existence of a good and all-powerful God. Therefore, God does not exist.

This objection has great intellectual power but it also has tremendous emotional power. It is when we suffer that we struggle to believe in a good and all-powerful God. It is when we burn with anger over such horrors as the rape of a family member, what took place in Auschwitz decades ago, or the news of another school shooting, that we are most sharply confronted by the problem of evil.

In his novel *The Brothers Karamazov*, Fyodor Dostoevsky forces us to feel the intellectual and emotional weight of this question. In the story, Ivan Karamazov confronts his younger Christian brother, Alyosha, with the atrocity of evil. Ivan declares,

> ...people speak sometimes about the "animal" cruelty of man, but that is terribly unjust and offensive to animals, no animal could ever be so cruel as a man, so artfully, so artistically cruel. A tiger simply gnaws and tears, that is all he can do. It would never occur to him to nail people by their ears overnight, even if he were able to do it.[1]

---

[1] Fyodor Dostoevsky, *The Brothers Karamazov*, trans Richard Pevear and Larissa Volokhonsky (New York: Everyman's Library Alfred A. Knopf Publishing, 1990), 238.

Ivan then tells a story about a little girl whose father and mother hate her.

> These educated parents subjected the poor five-year-old girl to every possible torture. They beat her, flogged her, kicked her, not knowing why themselves, until her whole body was nothing but bruises; finally they attained the height of finesse: in the freezing cold, they locked her all night in the outhouse, because she wouldn't ask to get up and go in the middle of the night (as if a five-year-old child sleeping its sound angelic sleep could have learned to ask by that age) - for that they smeared her face with her excrement and made her eat the excrement, and it was her mother, her mother who made her! And this mother could sleep while her poor little child was moaning all night in that vile place! Can you understand that a small creature, who cannot even comprehend what is being done to her, in a vile place, in the dark and the cold, beats herself on her strained little chest with her tiny fist and weeps with her anguished, gentle, meek tears for "dear God" to protect her – can you understand such nonsense, my friend and my brother, my godly and humble novice, can you understand why this nonsense is needed and created?[2]

In Matthew 13 Jesus tells a parable that has come to be known as "the parable of the wheat and the weeds." Here Jesus addresses many of our intellectual and emotional struggles with the problem of evil.

> The kingdom of heaven is like a man who sowed good seed in his field. But while everyone was sleeping, his enemy came and sowed weeds among the wheat, and went away. When the wheat sprouted and formed heads, then the weeds also appeared. The owner's servants came to him and said, "Sir, didn't you sow

---

[2] Dostoevsky, *The Brothers Karamazov,* 242.

good seed in your field? Where then did the weeds come from?" "An enemy did this," he replied." The servants asked him, "Do you want us to go and pull them up?" "No," he answered, "because while you are pulling the weeds, you may root up the wheat with them. Let both grow together until the harvest. At that time I will tell the harvesters: First collect the weeds and tie them in bundles to be burned; then gather the wheat and bring it into my barn."[3]

Jesus' parable speaks to our struggle with the problem of evil by teaching us three truths. First, good and evil exist (chapter 17). Second, good and evil will coexist in this life (chapter 18). Finally, good will always exist but evil will eventually cease to exist (chapter 19).

---

[3] Matthew 13:24-30.

Chapter 17
Good And Evil Exist

The first truth that Jesus states in his parable is that good and evil exist. This may seem so self-evident that it is hardly worth mentioning but, as we will see, it is actually quite profound.

The parable of the wheat and the weeds is, on one level, a rather basic parable about good and evil. Jesus speaks of a good farmer who sows good seed and an evil enemy who sneaks in to sow weeds among the wheat. This weed is likely a darnel plant, which was the annoyance of every farmer in the Middle East. It looks similar to wheat and entangles its roots with the wheat. Both of these factors make selective weeding difficult, if not impossible.

What does this parable mean? Jesus gives the interpretation of his parable in Matthew 13:37-39:

> He answered, "The one who sowed the good seed is the Son of Man. The field is the world, and the good seed stands for the sons of the kingdom. The weeds are the sons of the evil one, and the enemy who sows them is the devil. The harvest is the end of the age, and the harvesters are angels."

At the most basic level, Jesus is saying good and evil are both realities in this world. There is wheat and there are weeds.

In Matthew 13:27 the harvesters ask a question – likely the same question we are asking: "Where did the weeds come from?" In other words, where did evil come from? Jesus gives his answer in the next verse when he simply states, "An enemy did this."[1] Jesus then identifies this enemy as "the devil."[2] Evil, the Bible says, did not originate in God, for God is absolute goodness. Rather, evil is attributed to the enemy of God who is called the devil.

It may not seem like it, but Jesus' simple affirmation of the existence of both good and evil is an extremely satisfying start to engaging the problem of evil. In fact, it is miles ahead of other answers people have given. You see it is not just the Christian who has to face the problem of evil. When anyone tries to describe where evil comes from, it quickly becomes evident that everyone has to face the problem of evil. To demonstrate, let's consider two common answers people give for the existence of evil and show how, compared to Jesus, they are far less satisfying on an intellectual and an emotional level.

THE FAILURE OF ATHEISM TO ACCOUNT FOR EVIL

The first answer some people give for the existence of evil is to say that it proves God does not exist. This is the answer of the atheist. At first glance, it seems that evil in the world does indeed provide a powerful case against the existence of a good God. Upon further reflection, however, it becomes clear that atheists, not just Christians also have to face the problem of evil.

---

[1] Matthew 13:28.
[2] Matthew 13:39.

Let's begin where there is agreement. In reading the works of modern atheists it is abundantly clear that they believe certain actions are good while others are evil. They emphasize the fact that they are not moral relativists. Atheistic writings attack things like racism and the oppression of women as evil, while also upholding things like generosity and compassion as good. When atheists say they believe certain actions are good and others are evil, we have no reason to doubt their assertions or to question if they act in moral ways.

However, we must question the source of their categories of good and evil. Let's use an example. I am guessing we all agree that selling a seven year old girl into the sex trade is an evil act. But why is it evil? Do we simply mean that it is evil because it goes against our personal preference? No, we believe it is evil regardless if a person prefers it or not. Is the slavery and coercion of such a girl evil because our culture has said so? No, evil is not culturally defined; we believe abusing little girls is wrong in every culture from Thailand to Tanzania, Canada to Cambodia. Perhaps, then, evil is something that has evolved over time so that our world today has come to a general consensus? Here, also, we cannot agree, for this means that good and evil are ever-changing concepts. If this is the case, then we must say there could have been a time (hypothetically speaking) when it was a good thing to abuse little girls. Furthermore, this means our moral intuitions are always evolving and therefore it could be that our present convictions on this issue are wrong and a future generation will see things differently. However, we cannot accept this premise because we believe it always has been, presently is, and always will be wrong to sexually abuse little girls. This standard transcends personal preference, cultural bias, and time itself. It does not matter if some pimps in Thailand do not acknowledge it; we believe this is a universal standard by which all people must abide.

I am very glad to hear atheists condemning a horror as we have just discussed. But here is the crux of the matter: to reiterate, where do atheists get these absolute categories of good and evil? It is easy to see how a Christian can say the abuse of a little girl is evil, for a Christian believes God is good and just and has forbidden such acts. But where does the atheist get such absolute categories? Did the Big Bang explode certain moral commands into existence such as "Be generous" and "Be compassionate?" If the material universe is all that exists, what is the origin of concepts like good and evil? I will let Dawkins explain:

> Think about it. On one planet, and possibly only one planet in the entire universe, molecules that would normally make nothing more complicated than a chunk of rock, gather themselves into chunks of rock-sized matter of such staggering complexity that they are capable of running, jumping, swimming, flying, seeing, hearing, capturing and eating other such animated chunks of complexity; capable in some cases of thinking and feeling, and falling in love with yet other chunks of complex matter.[3]

If we are nothing more than complicated chunks of rock, it is difficult to see how our actions can be morally right or wrong. No one holds a boulder morally accountable for falling on and crushing another boulder. But we don't believe that a man abusing a girl is simply a collision of rocks (no matter how complicated the rocks may be). We hold such a man to be morally accountable and yet, if we live in an impersonal material universe, it is hard to see why the actions of complex rocks should be considered morally good or evil.

---

[3] Dawkins, *The God Delusion*, 411.

This discussion is strikingly portrayed in a film entitled *The Quarrel*. Two men, Hersh and Chaim, grew up together, but were estranged after an argument about God and evil. Their village and family were destroyed in World War II and each believed the other was dead. After surviving the Holocaust, they serendipitously meet in a park in Montreal and once again pick up their debate. Hersh has now become a rabbi and he offers a challenge to the secular Chaim.

> If a person does not have the Almighty to turn to, if there's nothing in the universe that's higher than human beings, then what's morality? Well, it's a matter of opinion. I like milk; you like meat. Hitler likes to kill people; I like to save them. Who's to say which is better? Do you begin to see the horror of this? If there is no Master of the universe, then who's to say that Hitler did anything wrong? If there is no God, then the people that murdered your wife and kids did nothing wrong.

We must be clear at this point, because this argument is continually misunderstood and misrepresented. We are not saying atheists are incapable of acting in moral ways; they most certainly can act morally. Neither are we saying atheists don't believe certain actions are good while others are evil; they do. Furthermore, we are not saying atheists have no moral compass; their rage against many forms of injustice proves they do. The point is this: *atheism, when followed to its logical end, has no categories for absolute good and evil.* Since atheists deny the existence of an Absolute, it follows that there can be no universal or absolute standards for human beings. Oh yes, it is very possible for us to make up our own rules but consistency would then require an atheist to say, "It is my view that abusing a girl is wrong, but since there are no universal absolutes, you are free to have your own opinion and I won't impose my opinion on you." Atheists, therefore, have a substantial problem with evil because, on the one hand, they want to use Christian categories of universal absolutes and yet, on the other hand, they want to deny that such absolutes exist.

To put it another way, if there is no God, then nothing can ultimately be "evil." For something to be defined as evil it must be contrasted to an ultimate standard of good. Without God, there can be no ultimate standard of good and therefore nothing can ultimately be called "evil."[4] Think of it this way: counterfeit money is only called "counterfeit" because there is such a thing as real money. If there were no such thing as real money it would be illogical to speak about counterfeit money. You can't have a counterfeit without the real thing.[5] Atheists want to speak about the reality of evil (counterfeit money) but they deny the existence of absolute Good (real money).

The best atheists have recognized that, without God, there can be no absolute good or evil. Richard Dawkins writes, "The universe we observe has precisely the properties we should expect if there is at bottom no design, no purpose, *no evil, no good,* nothing but blind pitiless indifference."[6] In light of this, Dawkins asks the right question: "If we reject Deuteronomy and Leviticus (as all enlightened moderns must do) by what criteria do we then decide which of religion's moral values to *accept?*"[7] What criteria indeed? That is the right question, for if human beings are the ones who determine what is good and evil, then it all boils down to a matter of personal taste, what

---

[4] The sixth century philosopher Boethius put it like this: "If God does indeed exist, what is the source of evil? But if he does not exist, what is the source of good?" The Christian may have a problem of evil but the atheist has a problem of evil *and* a problem of good. Boethius, *The Consolation of Philosophy* trans P.G. Walsh (Oxford: Oxford University Press, 1999), 11.
[5] This illustration borrowed from my friend Jon Morrison in *Clear Minds & Dirty Feet: A Reason to Hope, a Message to Share* (Abbotsford: Apologetics Canada Publishing, 2013), 178.
[6] Richard Dawkins, *Rivers Out Of Eden: A Darwinian View of Life* (New York: Basic Books, 1995), 133. Emphasis mine.
[7] Dawkins, *The God Delusion*, 81. Emphasis in original.

---

our culture thinks, or who has the power to impose their views on everyone else.

Frederick Nietzsche, the most famous atheist of the late 19th century, saw the implications of consistent atheism far more clearly than Dawkins. Nietzsche is the one who famously said, "God is dead." By this he meant that western civilization had killed God, not in the sense of literally murdering him, but in the sense that it had abandoned Christian truth. Although Nietzsche was happy to get rid of God and Christianity, he was terrified at the logical consequences of such an action. In his *Parable of the Madman* Nietzsche shows that getting rid of God is like getting rid of the sun; the planets of our lives no longer have an ultimate standard of good around which to orbit. Nietzsche understood that western civilization was built on Judeo-Christian values like honesty, love, justice, and kindness. People may not have always followed these values, but it was generally agreed that these were absolute standards that should be followed because God is honest, God is love, God is just, and God is kind. However, if we get rid of God, then there is no reason for people to continue keeping upholding these values, and civilization is in danger of plunging into chaos.

In Nietzsche's parable, a man carrying a lantern goes into a town square in the bright morning hours. He declares that he is looking for God. The atheists of the town ridicule him, but the man launches into a passionate diatribe about how the people have not realized the magnitude of killing God or the consequences of their actions.

> The madman jumped into their midst and pierced them with his eyes. "Whither is God?" he cried; "I will tell you. We have killed him---you and I. All of us are his murderers. But how did we do this? How could we drink up the sea? Who gave us the sponge to wipe away the entire horizon? What were we doing when we unchained this earth from its sun? Whither is it moving now?

Whither are we moving? Away from all suns? Are we not plunging continually? Backward, sideward, forward, in all directions? Is there still any up or down? Are we not straying, as through an infinite nothing?"[8]

The madman then smashes his lantern in frustration, declaring that he has come too soon. The villagers (the other atheists of Nietzsche's day and, by extension, our day) will need more time to realize the implications of what they have done. Nietzsche is calling us to realize that the logical end of getting rid of God means we must also get rid of absolute standards of good and evil. The end result is that individuals and societies are free to determine morality for themselves.

Again, I am grateful that the atheists of our day do not follow their atheism to its logical conclusion. This does not, however, change the fact that atheism cannot account for evil. If there is no God, then there is ultimately no such thing as good or evil – there is just human-made definitions that can change, depending on personal preference, culture, and time.

Jesus' truth, however, brings a measure of intellectual and emotional satisfaction because Jesus affirms what we already believe and feel in the core of who we are, namely, that good and evil are real.

THE FAILURE OF ILLUSION TO ACCOUNT FOR EVIL

The second answer people give for the existence of evil is to say it is merely an illusion. Scientology, Buddhism, some forms of Hinduism, and Christian Science teach that suffering and evil are merely an illusion; if we could see reality for what it truly is we would know this truth. But this only takes it back one step,

---

[8] http://www.fordham.edu/halsall/mod/nietzsche-madman.asp

for we should then ask, "Why would a good God allow us to live under an illusion?"

The real problem, however, is that we know evil is not an illusion; when we suffer we know in the depths of our being that evil is hideously real. To say otherwise is a slap in the face of the one who suffers. Again, Jesus' starting point is more satisfying because he takes evil seriously. The Bible never tires of denouncing the reality of evil. According to the Bible, evil is a parasite and a perversion of the good. Although God permits evil and even uses it, evil does not arise from his character. "God is light and in him there is no darkness at all"[9] and "God cannot be tempted by evil, nor does he tempt anyone."[10]

SUMMARY

So, unlike those who see evil as an illusion and unlike atheists who talk about good and evil but cannot provide a rationale for their existence, Jesus takes evil seriously by affirming its hideous reality. In the next chapter we will begin to work out the practical implications of Jesus' teaching on good and evil.

---

[9] 1 John 1:5.
[10] James 1:13.

Chapter 18
Good And Evil Will Coexist In This Life

If we are going to understand the Christian answer to the problem of evil we must take some time to really understand Jesus' teaching in the parable of the wheat and the weeds. Having affirmed the reality of good and evil, Jesus now offers a second truth: good and evil will coexist in this life. Understanding this truth is what can spare us from a *naïve optimism* that thinks that this evil world can be turned into utopia and from a *despairing pessimism* that thinks this evil world can never experience true change.

THE ALREADY BUT NOT YET OF THE KINGDOM

Jesus begins his parable by saying, "the kingdom of heaven is like..."[1] In order to appreciate the parable (and thus, Jesus' teaching on good and evil) we need to understand some background on the biblical idea of "the kingdom." Throughout

---

[1] Matthew 13:23.

the Old Testament, God promised that he would send a king who would set up a kingdom on the earth; a future kingdom that will wipe out all other evil kingdoms and usher in a glorious future age when there will be no evil, sickness, or death. Daniel 2:45, for instance, promises that, "The God of heaven will set up a kingdom that will never be destroyed, nor will it be left to another people. It will crush all those kingdoms and bring them to an end, but it will itself endure forever."

You can imagine the hype when Jesus stepped onto the scene and said, "The time has come...The kingdom of God is near."[2] Jesus taught that God's future kingdom had come in him. The evidence for this great claim is found in the fact that wherever Jesus went, he destroyed evil and its awful effects. Jesus cast out evil spirits, healed the sick, and raised the dead. Yet the people grew increasingly frustrated because Jesus did not crush the Romans. Evil continued and then, to make matters worse, Jesus was crucified. What else could this mean but that evil had defeated Jesus? What happened to the promised kingdom? The Bible answers that the cross was actually the victory of Jesus over evil; that in his resurrection Jesus defeated death itself, and that Jesus now reigns at the right hand of God as the conquering king. But this only makes the question of evil more forceful. If Jesus has conquered evil, why does evil still exist? If the kingdom is already here why do people fly airplanes into buildings and why do teenagers shoot their classmates?

Jesus' answer is that although the kingdom is already here, it has not yet fully come. Theologians call this "the already but not yet" of the kingdom. Jesus says that the future kingdom God promised has broken into the present through him, but that there is a time of overlap between this present evil age and the perfect future age to come. During this overlapping time Jesus says that God will allow the wheat and the weeds to grow

---

[2] Mark 1:15.

together. This will be a time when good and evil will coexist: "The servants asked him, 'Do you want us to go and pull them up?' 'No,' he answered, 'because while you are pulling the weeds, you may root up the wheat with them. *Let both grow together until the harvest.*' "[3]

Two analogies may help clarify the "already but not yet" of the kingdom clearer. First, it is like the difference between D-Day and V-E Day in World War II. On D-Day, June 6, 1944, the Allied nations won the critical battle of WWII when they invaded Normandy (think *Saving Private Ryan*). Even though Hitler was beaten, he did not surrender. In fact, some of the fiercest fighting took place after D-Day in conflicts like the Battle of the Bulge. On V-E Day (Victory in Europe Day) Germany officially surrendered. The guns were silenced and the war was over.

In the Bible's story, D-Day is the kingdom's invasion of enemy occupied territory through the life, death, and resurrection of Jesus. Although the decisive victory has been won, Jesus teaches in the parable of the wheat and the weeds that there will be a period of time before V-E Day – that is to say before he returns. The Bible teaches that in Jesus the kingdom has come but it has not yet fully come.[4]

Second, the present evil age and the future perfect age are like relay runners passing a baton. There is always a brief time when the two run alongside each other. In the same way, the future kingdom has already come (that baton has been passed) but it is not yet fully here (the old age still runs beside it). Jesus says we live in the time of overlap when the kingdom is here but not yet fully present. The old age is still running alongside.

---

[3] Matthew 13:28-30. Emphasis mine.
[4] Illustration from Oscar, Cullmann, *Christ and Time: The Primitive Christian Conception of Time and History* (Philadelphia: Westminster Press, 1964).

NAÏVE OPTIMISIM & DESPAIRING PESSIMISM

Understanding the "already but not yet" of the kingdom, and embracing Jesus' vision of good and evil, can save us from responding to evil with naïve optimism or despairing pessimism.

Some people seem to have a naïve optimism that the world is getting better and better and we will soon achieve utopia. I will never forget watching the media coverage when President Obama was elected for the first time in 2008. The media and the general public spoke of Obama in messianic terms - as if he were the one who would lead America, and even the world, into a glorious future. I remember thinking that no person could ever live up to the expectations people were placing on him. Regardless of how positively a person may view Obama, he has *not* ushered in a golden age. Jesus' teaching shows us that we must not be naïve and think utopia will come through a political leader, through better education, or through more knowledge in scientific endeavours. Jesus decrees that the wheat and the weeds will coexist until the end of time because the kingdom has not yet fully come.

Embracing Jesus and his teaching can also save us from a despairing pessimism, an attitude that says we cannot do anything about injustice, war, broken marriages, or poverty. The Christian teaching, however, is that change *can* happen because the kingdom has come in the risen and reigning Jesus. This is why in the midst of great evil and dark days, the Christian prays, "Your kingdom come...on earth as it is in heaven"[5] and then gets up from prayer and works hard in the belief that, since Jesus reigns, change is possible.

---

[5] Matthew 6:10.

SUMMARY

In this chapter I have presented Jesus' answer for how a Christian can believe in a good God and yet still acknowledge that the world is filled with evil. Jesus teaches that God's future kingdom of justice, perfect peace, and goodness has already arrived with his coming. However, Jesus teaches that the kingdom has not yet fully come. There is a time of overlap between the inauguration of the kingdom and its consummation. As we turn now to consider the future coming of the kingdom, we will discover Jesus' ultimate answer to the problem of evil.

Chapter 19
Good Will Always Exist
But Evil Will Cease To Exist

Good and evil exist. Good and evil will coexist in this life. Jesus' third truth gives the Bible's final answer to the problem of evil: good will always exist, but evil will eventually cease to exist. Jesus says, "Let both grow together until the harvest. At that time I will tell the harvesters: 'First collect the weeds and tie them in bundles to be burned; then gather the wheat and bring it into my barn.' "[1] Jesus then gives the interpretation:

> The harvest is the end of the age, and the harvesters are angels. As the weeds are pulled up and burned in the fire, so it will be at the end of the age. The Son of Man will send out his angels, and they will weed out of his kingdom everything that causes sin and all who do evil. They will throw them into the fiery furnace, where there will be weeping and gnashing of teeth. Then the righteous will shine like the sun in the kingdom of their Father. He who has ears, let him hear.[2]

---

[1] Matthew 13:30.
[2] Matthew 13:39-43.

Jesus says a day is coming when God's kingdom will fully come. On that day, Jesus declares he will rid the universe of all that is evil – "they will weed out of his kingdom everything that causes sin and all who do evil."[3] The Bible goes on to teach that on that day the devil, that enemy of God who filled this world with evil, will be "thrown into the lake of burning sulfur...[and] will be tormented day and night for ever and ever."[4] With evil destroyed, the Bible teaches that God will come and dwell among his people and "He will wipe every tear from [our] eyes. There will be no more death or mourning or crying or pain, for the old order of things has passed away."[5]

It is like the story of Robin Hood. The kingdom of England rightfully belonged to King Richard. While he was away at war, evil began to dominate the land through the wicked prince John. At times it was so bad it seemed King Richard had lost his kingdom. Suddenly Richard returned, crushed his enemies, and restored peace to the land. In a manner of speaking, this is the story of the Bible. In this parable Jesus says that his kingdom is already here and that he is the rightful king. He also asserts that "V-E Day" is coming when he will suddenly return, crush the wicked prince, and bring eternal joy to the citizens of his kingdom.

We have seen that Christianity certainly does have a challenge with the existence of evil. However, Christianity also has a solution for evil, namely, that God will utterly destroy it forever. The baton has been passed. Soon this present evil age will fall away and the perfect age will race into the eternal future. Those in Jesus' kingdom will experience eternal gladness in the presence of the good King. Never again will Jesus'

---

[3] Matthew 13:41.
[4] Revelation 20:10.
[5] Revelation 21:4.

people be afflicted by evil for "the righteous will shine like the sun in the kingdom of their Father."[6]

LONGING FOR A WORLD FREE OF EVIL

We had just finished watching Disney's movie *Frozen*, and my nine-year-old daughter was bursting with joy at another story that ended happily ever after. Still savouring the joy, we talked about why such stories resonate in our hearts. They ignite a sense of hope that, no matter how dark the pages of our stories become, things will turn out in the end. But is such hope realistic or is it mere wishful thinking? When the movie ends and we walk back into the trials of real life, is there any reason to hope in a "happily ever after"?

Before he became a Christian, C.S. Lewis struggled deeply with this question. Lewis, who went on to become the chair of Mediaeval and Renaissance Literature at Cambridge University, enjoyed the great mythical stories of history. He could not, however, reconcile the deep feelings these imaginary worlds evoked with real life in which he believed there was no God and thus no "happily every after." He wrote, "Nearly all that I loved I believed to be imaginary; nearly all that I believed to be real I thought grim and meaningless."[7] Troubled by this tension, he called the happily ever after stories, "lies breathed through silver."[8] Yet Lewis could not escape the fact that, somehow and in some way, these stories resonated as truth in his inmost being.

---

[6] Matthew 13:33.

[7] C.S. Lewis, *Surprised by Joy: The Shape Of My Early Life* (Orlando: Harcourt Inc., 1955), 170.

[8] Preserved in Tolkien's poem "Mythopoeia" and quoted in "On Fairy-Stories."

Everything changed one evening when Lewis went for a walk with his friend J.R.R. Tolkien (the author of the *The Lord of the Rings* and *The Hobbit*). As a Christian, Tolkien suggested that Lewis needed to rethink his views on the myths he loved. He suggested that, "The best myths…are not deliberately constructed falsehoods, but are rather tales woven by people to capture the echoes of deeper truths. Myths offer a fragment of that truth, not its totality. They are like splintered fragments of the true light."[9]

Tolkien went on to explain that there is one "true myth" to which all the other myths point. This true myth is the historical story of what God has done for us in Jesus Christ. Like all good stories, it seems that all is lost as evil wreaks havoc through God's world. Yet it ends in what Tolkien called "eucatastrophe" - a turn of events that results in the joyous consolation of a happily ever after.[10]

> The Gospels contain a fairy-story, or a story of a larger kind which embraces all the essence of fairy-stories…and among its marvels is the greatest and most complete conceivable eucatastrophe…But this story has entered History…There is no tale ever told that men would rather find was true.[11]

Tolkien's point is that all the great fairy stories are pointers to the one true story of Christ that culminates in the Great Eucatastrophe when Christ returns and destroys evil. This critical change in Lewis' thinking soon led him to become a Christian. Lewis now saw that the imaginary stories he loved,

---

[9] Alistair McGrath, *C.S. Lewis – A Life: Eccentric Genius, Reluctant Prophet* (Illinois: Tyndale House Publishers, 2013), Kindle Edition, Location 2457.
[10] Tolkien coined this term by adding the Greek prefix "eu" (meaning "good") to "catastrophe" (traditionally understood in literature to refer to the unraveling or conclusion of the story's plot.
[11] Tolkien, Christopher, ed., *The Monsters and the Critics and Other Essays* (London: George Allen and Unwin, 1983), 155-156.

though not the whole truth, were not merely lies. They were simply fragments of truth that pointed to the one great truth found in Jesus Christ.

HOW THE GREAT STORIES POINT TO JESUS

Walking home with my daughter after watching the movie, I said, "The reason why *Frozen* resonates so much with your heart is because it is a small version of God's big story. Just as Arendelle was under a curse, our world is also under the curse of sin. Just as true love's kiss was not enough of an act of true love to break the curse of winter in Arendelle, so also the curse of sin in our world cannot be broken simply by people trying harder to love each other. And just as the curse was broken when Anna sacrificially laid down her life for her sister, so also Jesus, in the greatest act of true love, sacrificed his life for us that the curse might be broken. For Anna's act she was given back her life. So also, God raised Jesus from the dead and promises to one day bring us into a new world where everything is the way it's supposed to be."

All the great stories mirror to this idea. There is a Prince who, like in *Sleeping Beauty*, has slain the dragon that holds us captive. There is a place where, like in *Peter Pan*, we will never grow old. There is hero, who like in all the superhero stories, will utterly vanquish evil. There is Prince who, like in *Cinderella*, has taken us from rags to the riches of being his bride. There is a day coming when, like Frodo in *The Lord of the Rings*, we will end our journey in the east and the ships will come to carry us home to the undying lands in the West, where white shores call and all turns to silver glass. Christians can enjoy these stories and, when they are done, say to each other, "Because of what

God has done for us in Jesus, we will get all of this and far more."[12]

Christians believe that our longing for the world to be put right is not mere wishful thinking, or, worse, the naïve thoughts of children living in a fantasy world. We believe these longings are the ancient echoes of Eden within our souls – that through Jesus, God is working everything together toward a day when his kingdom will restore – even exceed - what was lost in this world so filled with evil. When the kingdom fully comes, good will exist forever but evil will cease to exist in God's universe.

HOPE IN THE DARKNESS

Christianity offers a message of hope to people struggling in a world filled with evil. This message begins by affirming the reality of good and evil and taking both realities seriously. Christianity then gives a framework for understanding the existence of evil as well as the existence of a good God. This framework is Jesus' teaching on the "already but not yet" of the kingdom of God. Finally, the Christian message promises that a day is coming when Jesus will return, destroy evil, set up his good kingdom on earth, and give it to all who are children of his kingdom.

It is this hope of a "happily ever after" that provides strength when the pages of our own stories grow dark with trials and hardship.

> It's like in the great stories, Mr. Frodo. The ones that really mattered. Full of darkness and danger they were. And

---

[12] The above part of this paragraph is inspired by Timothy Keller who has often spoken of various movies and stories in a manner similar to what I have done here.

---

sometimes you didn't want to know the end. Because how could the end be happy? How could the world go back to the way it was when so much bad had happened? But in the end, it's only a passing thing, this shadow. Even darkness must pass. A new day will come. And when the sun shines, it will shine out the clearer. Those were the stories that stayed with you. That meant something, even if you were too small to understand why.[13]

---

[13] Samwise Gamgee in *The Lord of the Rings: The Two Towers* Directed by Peter Jackson (New Line Cinemas, 2002), DVD.

PROBLEM #6:
LOVE & HELL

HOW CAN A LOVING GOD
SEND PEOPLE TO HELL?

INTRODUCTION

The vast majority of people in the world believe in God. This is true even in secular countries like Canada. Even though my home province of British Columbia is the least conventionally religious in all of Canada, it does not follow that the majority of people are atheists, or even agnostics. Pollster Reginald Bibby states that 14% of people claim to be atheists while the vast majority of British Columbians claim to believe in God.[1] When asked what God is like, most will say God is loving and accepting of all people. It is, therefore, extremely jarring to people when Christianity speaks about both a loving God and the existence of hell. How could a loving God possibly send people to hell? To many people, the number one problem with Christianity is its teaching on hell.

The goal of these next few chapters is *not* to convince you to like hell or to think it is a nice place, for the Bible never suggests or requires this. I do, however, want to explore how the Bible brings together what we often separate; namely, a God of love and the existence of a place called hell.

It may surprise you to learn that the majority of the Bible's teaching about hell does not come from the Old Testament, which many people think of as portraying a God of wrath. Neither does it come from Paul or Luke whose writings make up the bulk of the New Testament. The majority of the Bible's teaching about hell comes from Jesus himself. This is quite shocking since Jesus is widely considered to be the most loving person who ever lived. Even individuals whom our culture upholds as examples of love, like Mother Theresa and Ghandi,

---

[1] Douglas Todd, *Cascadia the Elusive Utopia (Exploring the Spirit of the Pacific Northwest)* (Vancouver: Ronsdale Press, 2008), 12.

expressly taught that Jesus was far more loving than themselves. Ghandi, for instance, wrote of Jesus' perfect love: "A man who was completely innocent, offered himself as a sacrifice for the good of others, including his enemies, and became the ransom of the world. It was a perfect act."[2] The fact that it is Jesus who spoke most about hell should give us pause to consider if, perhaps, we have misunderstood the entire subject.

In these next few chapters, I will focus on John 3:16, which contains arguably the most famous words Jesus ever spoke. Here, the most loving person who ever lived speaks about both the love of God and the existence of hell. It is love, however, that is emphasized most since Jesus' teaching about hell is set within the broader context of God's love. In other words, Jesus will not allow us to discuss hell without also considering the love of God in sending Jesus to rescue us from hell and bring us into a life of eternal bliss.

In his teaching about hell, Jesus reveals three aspects of God's love. In chapter 20 we will discover a love that warns. In chapter 21 we will contemplate a love that is fair. Finally, in chapter 22 we will reflect on a love that rescues.

---

[2] M.K. Ghandi, *Ghandi and Communal Problems* (Mumbai: Centre for Study Of Society and Secularism), chapter 25. http://www.mkgandhi.org /ebks/Gandhi_communalproblems.pdf (accessed April 10, 2015).

Chapter 20
A Love That Warns

A man who realizes in any measure the awful force of the words eternal hell *won't shut up about it, but will speak with all tenderness.*[1]

- A.A. Hodge

For God so loved the world that he gave his one and only Son, that whoever believes in him shall not perish but have eternal life.

- Jesus in John 3:16

Some years ago, a dense fog shrouded a major highway a few miles south of London. At 6:15am, a semi-truck carrying huge rolls of paper was involved in a major accident, colliding with dozens of cars and killing ten people. A police car arrived on the scene and two policemen ran back up the highway to stop oncoming traffic. They waved their arms and shouted as loudly as they could, but most drivers took no notice and raced on to the inevitable disaster ahead of them. The policemen picked up

---

[1] Cited in Ligon Duncan III, "Speaking Soberly and Sensitively About Hell," *Modern Reformation Magazine* 11, no. 3 (May/June 2002): 22.

traffic cones and flung them at the car's windshields in a desperate attempt to warn drivers of the danger. One policeman told how tears streamed down his face as car after car went by and he waited for the sickening sound of impact as they hit the growing mass of wreckage beyond.[2]

Jesus, the most loving person who ever lived, raises the topic of hell not to intimidate us but to lovingly warn us. When we find Jesus' words difficult to bear, we must realize that avoiding hell was one of the core themes in Jesus' core teaching. Jesus was not a wild-eyed fire-and-brimstone preacher who ranted and raved about how we are all going to burn. The very fact that Jesus speaks about hell reveals his love; to warn someone who is in imminent danger is an act of love. Not to do so is a sign of indifference and cruelty.

Jesus' warning occurs in the word "perish": "For God so loved the world that he gave his one and only Son, that whoever believes in him shall not *perish* but have eternal life." To "perish," in Jesus' teaching, does not mean people cease to exist when they die. To perish means to exist eternally in a place Jesus called, "hell." Jesus described hell in terrifying terms and images – a place of darkness, of weeping, of suffering, of anger and gnashing of teeth. Most alarming is Jesus' teaching that "to perish" is to have the face of God turned against a person in eternal judgment.[3] Michael Horton puts it like this:

> Hell is not ultimately about fire but about God. Whatever the exact nature of the physical punishments, the real terror awaiting the unrepentant is God himself and his inescapable

---

2 John Blanchard, *Whatever Happened to Hell?* (Durham, England: Evangelical Press, 1993), 297.
3 For Jesus' teaching that 1) Hell is real - see Mt 5:21-22, 27-30; 23:15, 33 2) Hell involves rejection – see Mt 7:23; 8:11-12; 22:13; 25:30 3) Hell involves pain – see Mt 13:30, 40-43, 49-50; 18:6-9; 24:51.

presence forever with his face turned against [the unrepentant].[4]

Contrary to popular opinion, Jesus does not describe hell as a place where people party and enjoy themselves. The Bible says all good things like laughter, music, food, drink, art, and sports are gifts that come from having God's face turned toward us in blessing. In hell, God's face is turned away and therefore all blessings like peace, happiness, and pleasure are removed. It is no wonder that when Dante wrote the *Inferno* he envisioned a sign chiseled above Hell's gate, which reads, "Abandon all hope, you who enter here."[5]

It is at this point, when we feel protest rising in our hearts, that we need to remind ourselves why Jesus said these words in John 3:16. Rather than leave us to perish, Jesus says God has set his love on us. The first way God showed his love was to send Jesus to warn us of the imminent danger toward which we are speeding. In a sense, John 3:16 is the traffic cone Jesus throws at the windshield of our lives. Out of deep love for us, Jesus waves his arms and shouts, "you will perish if you keep speeding on in your rebellion." There is no question that Jesus' teaching is hard to hear, graphic in its language, disturbing, and unsettling, but it is truly an act of love; love warns of danger.

While we may agree that it is a loving act to warn about hell, the heart of our objection lies in the fact that Jesus says hell exists. In other words, it just seems unfair for a loving God to send people to hell even if we are warned about it. This is what we will grapple with in the next chapter.

---

[4] Michael Horton, "Is Hell Separation From God?," *Modern Reformation Magazine* 11, no. 3 (May/June 2002): 19.
[5] Dante, Alighieri, *The Inferno*, trans. John Ciardi (New York: New American Library, 1982), Kindle Edition, Location 536.

Chapter 21
A Love That Is Fair

If there is a God who will damn his children forever, I would rather go to hell than to go to heaven and keep the society of such an infamous tyrant…I do not believe this doctrine; neither do you. If you did, you could not sleep one moment. Any man who believes it, and has within his breast a decent, throbbing heart, will go insane. A man who believes that doctrine and does not go insane has the heart of a snake, and the conscience of a hyena.[1]

- Robert Ingersoll (19th century atheist)

We get ourselves laughed at for proclaiming that God will one day judge the world.[2]

- Tertullian (4th century pastor)

Hell is not fair. This is the common response people have to Jesus' teaching. Most would agree with Bertrand Russell, the most famous atheist of the mid 20th century, when he wrote,

---

[1] Robert G. Ingersoll, *Works of Robert Ingersoll* (New York: Bibliobazaar, 2007), 182.
[2] Tertullian, "The Apology", ed. Alexander Roberts and James Donaldson in *Ante-Nicene Fathers* (Peabody: Hendrickson Publishers, 2004), 3:52.

"There is one serious defect to my mind in Christ's moral character, and that is that He believed in hell. I do not myself feel that any person who is really profoundly humane can believe in everlasting punishment."[3] In this chapter, I will show two ways in which Jesus demonstrates the fairness of hell.

HELL IS THE LOGICAL OUTCOME OF HUMAN FREEDOM

First, Jesus shows us that hell is fair because it is the logical outcome of human freedom. We can see this in Jesus' use of "world" in John 3:16: "For God so loved *the world* that he gave his one and only Son, that whoever believes in him shall not perish but have eternal life." In John's gospel "world" refers to "humanity in rebellion against God" or "humanity rejecting God." The Bible teaches that God created the first human beings, Adam and Eve, not as robots to mechanically obey his every command, but as free beings who could choose to love him or rebel against him.

In the book and movie *The Stepford Wives*, a group of men have perfect marriages because they have perfect wives who do whatever they say. The only problem is that their wives are actually robots. The story demonstrates how such love is not true love at all. In like manner, God created Adam and Eve to love him. However, they chose to use their freedom to rebel against God, to reject him, and to live for themselves. All of humanity has followed in their footsteps.

The thing to notice in John 3:16 is how Jesus connects "world" with "perish." According to Jesus, all of humanity is perishing because, as morally responsible beings, we have rejected our Creator. If people reject God in this life then, in one sense, he

---

[3] Bertrand Russell, *Why I Am Not a Christian* (London: Unwin Books, 1967), 22.

will give them what they want, namely, an eternity without God.

Think of it this way. Why would anyone who rejects God in this life want heaven when being in heaven means to be in the presence of God? Heaven will be eternal adoration of God but, if you don't adore God on earth, why would you want to adore him for eternity? Heaven will be eternal thankfulness and praise to Jesus for his sacrifice, but if you do not find Jesus and his work on our behalf to be the most glorious thing in the universe, why would you want to go there? Heaven will be eternal submission to God, but if you don't like the idea of obeying God on earth, why would you want to do this for eternity? In heaven, God's people will savour him forever like we savour honey melted on hot toast, but if you think God tastes more like Brussels sprouts (which you have disliked and avoided all your life) why would you want to savour God for all eternity?

In a sense, then, hell is simply the logical end of our choices about God. This is why C.S. Lewis wrote, "There are only two kinds of people in the end: those who say to God, 'Thy will be done,' and those to whom God says, in the end, '*Thy* will be done.' All that are in Hell, choose it."[4] Likewise, the Scottish pastor and author, George MacDonald, said, "The one principle of hell is: I am my own."[5] This is why Lewis also wrote, "I willingly believe that the damned are, in one sense, successful, rebels to the end; that the doors of Hell are locked on the *inside*."[6] Lewis does not mean people enjoy hell and want to remain there. He goes on to write, "I do not mean that the ghosts may not *wish* to come out of hell...but they certainly do not will even the first primary stages of that self-abandonment

---

[4] C.S. Lewis, *The Great Divorce* (New York: Simon & Schuster, 1996), 72. Emphasis in original.

[5] C.S, Lewis, *George MacDonald: An Anthology* (New York: MacMillan, 1948), 85.

[6] C.S. Lewis, *The Problem of Pain* (New York: Simon & Schuster, 1996), 114.

through which alone the soul can reach any good."[7] In other words, it is not that people want hell; it's just that they *don't want* God. If people want to live without God, then God will give them what they want for all eternity.

HELL IS THE LOGICAL OUTCOME OF GOD'S JUSTICE

Second, Jesus shows us that hell is fair because it is the logical outcome of God's justice. People say, "I believe in a God of love, not a God of judgment." Initially that sounds wonderful, but have you ever considered that a God who does not judge is not a loving God at all? Theologian J.I. Packer writes,

> The truth is that part of God's moral perfection is his perfection in judgment. Would a God who did not care about the difference between right and wrong be a good and admirable Being? Would a God who put no distinction between the beasts of history, the Hitlers and Stalins (if we dare use names), and His own saints, be morally praiseworthy and morally perfect? Moral indifference would be an imperfection in God, not a perfection. But not to judge the world would be to show moral indifference. The final proof that God is a perfect moral Being, not indifferent to questions of right and wrong, is the fact that he has committed himself to judge the world.[8]

We may say we don't believe in a God who judges, but in reality, we are always demanding that God act in judgement: "God, why don't you do something about all the evil in the world? Why don't you stop ISIS? Why don't you do something about kids being abused, CEO's stealing money, and governments killing their people?" When we talk like this we are saying, "I want a God who is just. I want a God who takes good and evil seriously and does something about it." This is

---

[7] Lewis, *The Problem of Pain*, 114.

[8] J.I. Packer, *Knowing God* (Downers Grove: InterVarsity Press, 1993), 143.

exactly what the existence of hell reveals - a God who takes good and evil seriously. Hell speaks to a God who will not allow people to get away with evil forever and who will, ultimately, ensure justice is done.

People who speak about a loving God who never judges anyone are so often those living comfortable pampered lives untouched by the atrocities of the world. When your government systematically kills your extended family (like in North Korea), or your own neighbours cut down your children with machetes (like what happened in Rwanda), you cry out for a God of justice. The same thing is true when you are personally touched by injustice. When your car is stolen, your house broken into, your sister date-raped, or your spouse cheats on you and then takes everything in the divorce, you cry out that life is not fair and you want someone (especially God) to do something about it.

The existence of hell reveals that we live in a universe that is ruled by a God who, thankfully, cares about justice. Just as any loving person feels a justified type of anger over injustice, so the God of love feels anger toward injustice. Becky Pippert writes,

> The Bible never suggests that God's anger is lightly provoked. Or that God is ready to pounce at the first misstep. On the contrary, we are told he is "slow to anger" (Exodus 34:6). And his anger does not come from having a bad temper. Indeed, God's anger issues from the intensity and depth of his love for us, as well as the height of his moral perfection and his outrage against evil...If God were not angry over how we are destroying ourselves, then he wouldn't be good and he wouldn't be loving. Anger isn't the opposite of love. Hate is,

and the final form of hate is indifference…To be truly good one has to be outraged by evil and utterly hostile to injustice.[9]

In one sense, then Jesus' teaching on hell should be a tremendous comfort to us. If we lived in a universe where there was no God and no life after death, then people would ultimately get away with every betrayal, murder, robbery, infidelity, and abusive act they committed. Jesus says we live in a universe ruled by a just God who cares so much about good and evil that *he will do something about it.*

GRACE TO THE UNDESERVING

Perhaps, just when we are starting to think there is some degree of fairness to Jesus' teaching on hell, we suddenly find our satisfaction turning to complaint. For Jesus does not say it is only the Hitlers and Stalins of the world who are perishing. According to Jesus, it is "the world" that is perishing and the world is *all* of humanity (including us) in rebellion against God.

Before we can even begin to protest or digress into a long debate about whether we truly deserve hell or not, Jesus hurries on to tell us the good news about what God has done about the fact that we are in danger of perishing. The most loving man who ever lived will not allow us to discuss his teaching on hell without ensuring that we also know how gracious God has been in providing a way of escape.

---

[9] Becky Pippert, 2nd ed. *Hope Has Its Reasons: The Search To Satisfy Our Deepest Longings* (Downers Grove: InterVarsity Press, 2009), Kindle Edition, Locations 1122, 1141, 1147.

Jesus' approach seems to me to be like the time I handed my dad a few hundred dollars and shamefully confessed that I had stolen from him throughout my childhood. He had every right to emphasize how wrong my actions were, to get angry with me, and to discipline me. To my great shock however, he followed up the conversation by saying, "Not only do I forgive you but I am going to credit this money to your student loan debt." Although Jesus does affirm the fact that we are all rebels against God and in danger of perishing, he does not dwell on this point. Rather, he rushes on to tell us what God has done about our hopeless condition. This is the subject of the final chapter.

Chapter 22
A Love That Rescues

Dr. Bryan Chapell tells the story from his hometown of two brothers who decided to play in the sand banks by the river. Since this town depends on the river for commerce, dredges regularly clear its channels of sand and dump the sand in great mounds along the river's edge. Nothing is more fun for children than playing in these mountainous sand piles – and few things are more dangerous.

The dredges dump the sand in piles on the shore while it is still wet. As a result, the outside of the pile dries, providing a rigid crust, but, large empty voids form inside as the water runs out of the pile. If a child climbs on a mound of sand that has this type of hidden void, the crust will easily collapse into the void. The sand from higher up will then quickly slide downwards to fill the void and thus trap the child.

This is exactly what happened to the two brothers as they raced up one of the larger mounds. When the boys did not return home at dinnertime, family and neighbours organized a search. When they located the younger brother, only his head and shoulders protruded from the mound. He was unconscious from the pressure of sand on his body. The searchers began digging frantically. When they had cleared the sand to his waist, he began to regain consciousness.

"Where is your brother?" the rescuers shouted.

"I'm standing on his shoulders," replied the child.

At the sacrifice of his own life the older brother had lifted the younger to safety and rescued him. [1]

It is a loving deed to warn someone in danger, but if you have the ability to help, love also requires action. Not to act when you have the ability to do so reveals a heart lacking love. When the most loving person who ever lived spoke about hell, he emphasized the fact that God has also acted on our behalf by giving the gift of his Son to the world that has rejected him: "For God so loved the world that *he gave his one and only Son*, that whoever believes in him shall not perish.

The Bible teaches that God is a Trinity of persons. This means there is only one God. Yet, this God exists in three equal yet distinct persons: the Father, the Son, and the Holy Spirit. Two thousand years ago the Father gave the world the gift of his Son. God the Son took on human flesh and was given the name "Jesus." Why did God become a man? Jesus' answer is clear: that we might "not perish." To further emphasize the point that he came to rescue us from perishing, Jesus explains himself in John 3:17: "For God did not send his Son into the world to condemn the world, but to save the world through him." Again, Jesus will not allow us to talk about hell without also talking about what God has done to rescue us from it.

The rest of the New Testament goes on to teach that Jesus rescues us from perishing through his life, death, resurrection, and ascension to the right hand of God. In his life, Jesus lived the obedient life that we should have lived but did not. In his death, Jesus died the death we should have died but won't. In a very real sense, Jesus faced hell on our behalf; he took our

---

[1] Bryan Chapell, *Each For The Other: Marriage as it's Meant to Be* (Grand Rapids: BakerBooks, 2006), 14-15.

punishment upon himself and was rejected by God. When God turned his face away, Jesus cried out, "My God, my God, why have you forsaken me?"[2] In his resurrection, Jesus conquered sin and death and victoriously ascended to the right hand of God where he ever lives to intercede for us.

Put another way, rebellious humanity was perishing under the sand of God's judgement. God would have been perfectly just to let us perish but, out of love for us, God sent Jesus to rescue us. Jesus, our true elder brother, went to the cross and there he placed us on his shoulders as the sand of the judgement that we deserved came down around him and took his life. Jesus will not allow the existence of hell to dominate the discussion. If we want to talk about Jesus' teaching on hell, then Jesus also requires us to talk about the love God has shown in warning us, in being fair toward us, and in rescuing us.

RESCUED *FROM* ETERNAL DEATH *FOR* ETERNAL LIFE

Jesus will also not let us discuss hell without giving thought to heaven: "For God so loved the world that he gave his one and only Son, that whoever believes in him shall not perish *but have eternal life.*" The God of love does not just rescue us from perishing; he rescues us *from* eternal perishing *for* eternal life.

All of us are searching for life. Every self-help book, every seminar on improving our lives, the millions we spend on vacations and entertainment, – all aimed at this one thing; namely, to find a deep happiness and joy that is fullness of life. Yet after trying so many experiences we end up singing with U2, "I still haven't found what I am looking for." Even when our joy is as full as it can get, like when we behold a perfect sunset or hold our newborn baby, we cannot hold on to the

---

[2] Matthew 27:46.

moment. The moment slips through our grasp so that we agree with the poet Wallace Stevens who wrote, "But even in contentment I feel the need of some imperishable bliss."[3] In John 3:16 Jesus is saying, "I came to give you the life you are longing for. You can't talk about hell unless you also talk about how I have done everything necessary to rescue you and give you an eternity of 'imperishable bliss.' "

In C.S. Lewis' *The Chronicles of Narnia*, children from this world enter the world of Narnia and experience amazing adventures. After seven books, the children die in a train crash but Aslan, the Creator of Narnia, takes them to a new world that is greater than Earth or Narnia. Lewis concludes the whole series with these words:

> And this is the end of all the stories, and we can most truly say that they lived happily ever after. But for them it was only the beginning of the real story. All of their life in this world and all their adventures in Narnia had only been the cover and the title page: now at last they were beginning Chapter One of the Great Story, which no one on earth has read: which goes on for ever: in which every chapter is better than the one before.[4]

WHAT WOULD YOU PAY FOR ETERNAL BLISS?

If all this is true – if hell and heaven are real and it is possible to escape the one and enjoy the other - we must ask, "What do I have to do to get it? What do I have to pay?" To our astonishment, we find Jesus saying God's rescue, leading to eternal life, is free. More accurately, it is free for us, but it certainly was not free for God. Our rescue and eternal joy cost God the life of his one and only Son.

---

[3] From a poem entitled *Sunday Morning*. http://www.poetryfoundation.org/poetrymagazine/poem/2464 (accessed Jan 28, 2015).
[4] C.S. Lewis, *The Final Battle* (New York: HarperCollins Publishers, 1984), 228.

There are two senses in which all of this is free to us. First, God's rescue from perishing for eternal bliss is free in the sense that it is not limited to a special group. It is free to all: "*whoever* believes in him shall not perish but have eternal life." There is tremendous love in the word "Whoever." A person cannot say, "I am so bad that God could never accept me." Jesus says, "Whoever." Neither can a person say, "I am too young or too old." Jesus says, "Whoever." A person cannot say, "Christianity is more of a western thing and I am eastern." Jesus says, "Whoever."

Second, and even more astonishingly, God's loving offer is free in the sense that people do not have to earn it. Jesus does not put a price on this invaluable gift of eternal life. This is what makes Christianity unique among the spiritual paths and religions of the world. All other paths say, "You have a problem and here is what you have to do to fix it." Christianity says, "You cannot do anything to stop yourself from perishing. But what you cannot do for yourself, God has done for you. He has done it all in giving Jesus to you, and all you have to do is receive the Rescuer."

HAVE WE GOTTEN OFF TRACK?

Are we getting off track? Wasn't the subject of these chapters supposed to be the offensiveness of Christianity's teaching on hell? If we are hearing Jesus correctly, it seems that the feeling of being off track is a clear indication that we are actually on the right track. The Bible's story, summarized in John 3:16, is not about how God wants everyone to burn in hell. It is about what God has done to rescue people from hell. Just as opening the blinds at noon banishes darkness to the smallest corners of a room, so Jesus intends for the blazing light of what God has done for us in Jesus to overcome the unsettling darkness that a discussion on hell provokes.

Afterword

It is my hope that *The Problem With Christianity* has enabled you to find some answers (on an intellectual, existential, and emotional level) to the six unsettling questions considered in this book.

Some readers may now realize that the obstacles that previously kept them from belief have fallen away, but are still unsure what belief in Jesus looks like. It begins by simply talking to God. Admit that you have rebelled against him, ask for mercy on the basis of Jesus' death, and ask God to help change you from living as a rebel to living as someone who loves Jesus as their ruler and King. You could pray something like this:

Dear God,

I know that I am not worthy to be accepted by you. I don't deserve your gift of eternal life. I am guilty of rebelling against you and ignoring you. I need forgiveness.

Thank you for sending your Son to die for me that I may be forgiven. Thank you that he rose from the dead to give me new life.

Please forgive me and change me, that I may live with Jesus as ruler and king. Amen.

I would be delighted to hear that someone (perhaps you) found the answers I have attempted to give in this book convincing enough to have prayed such a prayer. Regardless of your response, I value hearing from, and interacting with, my readers. If you would like to get in touch with me, please email theproblemwithchristianity@gmail.com.

Author Request

Although *The Problem With Christianity* is published through Apologetics Canada, I am responsible for most of its promotion. Since I cannot possibly reach all the people who would be interested in this book, I would appreciate your help in sharing it with your circle of influence. It would make a difference if you would consider the following:

1. Go to my website (see below) and subscribe to email updates about my book. This also enables me to notify you of future books I may write.
2. Post comments and share a link to my book's website on social media platforms like Facebook or Twitter.
3. Write a review on Amazon.com, Amazon.ca, and/or Goodreads.com.
4. Personally recommend my book to others.
5. Buy a few extra copies to give away as gifts.

Book website:
www.theproblemwithchristianity.com

Follow Barton's preaching:
www.centralbaptistchurch.ca

Follow Barton's blogging:
www.groundedinthegospel.com

Check out Apologetics Canada:
www.apologeticscanada.com

Author Bio

Barton Priebe was raised in British Columbia and southern Alberta. He worked as a Resident Director at Trinity Western University (1998-2002). After serving thirteen years (2002-2015) as the lead pastor of Dunbar Heights Baptist Church in Vancouver, Canada, he became the lead pastor of Central Baptist Church in Victoria, Canada. Barton is passionate about engaging deeply with others on all issues of faith and life. Barton and his wife Heather have four children. He is currently working on his Doctor of Ministry at Northwest Baptist Seminary.